*What people are saying about*

# NO OTHER GODS

"I have loved Kelly Minter as a songwriter, worship leader, and wise teacher, but now I love her as an amazing author. *No Other gods* is fresh writing, biblical truth, and vulnerable, story-driven application. This book just became the next book I have to get for everyone."

—ANGELA THOMAS, BEST-SELLING AUTHOR AND SPEAKER

"False gods. They're all around us, invading the crevices of our hearts and minds with such cunning maneuvers that we are often unaware of their presence. Thank the Lord for Kelly Minter. She unapologetically exposes the reality of modern-day idol worship in all of us. This book, combining her personal journey and the power of Scripture, should be read by every believer who is ready to live fully and whole-heartedly for the one true God."

—PRISCILLA SHIRER, AUTHOR AND SPEAKER

"With an engaging style and endearing vulnerability, Kelly Minter skillfully weaves timeless biblical truths together with practical, personal applications. Her words are sure to challenge and encourage many, no matter what their age or stage."

—JERUSHA CLARK, AUTHOR OF *EVERY THOUGHT CAPTIVE, INSIDE A CUTTER'S MIND*, AND *THE LIFE YOU CRAVE*

"In a time when Christian lives are becoming increasingly watered down, *No Other gods* reminds us of the one true God who is calling us into a relationship that is not only satisfying to our deepest longings, but also freeing to the secret parts of us that cry out for wholeness. This book inspires us to go to a depth of relationship with our Maker that is fresh and challenging."

—DEBBIE ALSDORF, FOUNDER OF DESIGN4LIVING MINISTRIES AND AUTHOR OF *DEEPER: LIVING IN THE REALITY OF GOD'S LOVE*

"With our current society so focused on discovering the next 'idol,' we are easily drawn into believing we can find fulfillment in fame, money, or success. In *No Other gods*, we come face-to-face with our own 'small gods' that we believe can give us true satisfaction. Through Kelly's authenticity in her own journey, we are invited to take inventory of our hearts and urged to let go of idols keeping us from embracing the one true God."

—CINDY WEST, DIRECTOR OF WORSHIP ARTS, WOODMEN VALLEY CHAPEL, AND AUTHOR OF *SAYING YES* (FORTHCOMING FROM DAVID C. COOK, FALL 2008)

"In *No Other gods*, Kelly Minter has written a beautiful, personal account of a "journey," the one we all take from time to time that seductively leads us away from peace in pursuit of things that cannot satisfy. By drawing light onto the unseen and often overlooked impediments of her own, Kelly bravely leads the charge on the many areas we all share in common; taking no prisoners along the way, she gently encourages us to wholeness by example. Fast paced, well-written, honest, and practical, *No Other gods* presents a bridge from where you are to where you could be. Great work."

—MARGARET BECKER, SONGWRITER AND AWARD-WINNING RECORDING ARTIST

# NO OTHER GODS

# NO OTHER GODS

## KELLY MINTER

David C Cook®

*transforming lives together*

NO OTHER GODS
Published by David C Cook
4050 Lee Vance View
Colorado Springs, CO 80918 U.S.A.

David C Cook Distribution Canada
55 Woodslee Avenue, Paris, Ontario, Canada N3L 3E5

David C Cook U.K., Kingsway Communications
Eastbourne, East Sussex BN23 6NT, England

The graphic circle C logo is a registered trademark of David C Cook.

The Web site addresses recommended throughout this book are offered as a resource to you.
These Web sites are not intended in any way to be or imply an endorsement on the part of
David C Cook, nor do we vouch for their content.

All Scripture quotations, unless otherwise noted, are taken from the *Holy Bible, New International Version*®.
*NIV*®. Copyright © 1973, 1978, 1984 by International Bible Society. Used by permission of Zondervan.
All rights reserved. Italics in Scripture quotations have been added by the author for emphasis. Scripture
quotations marked KJV are from the King James Version of the Bible. (Public Domain.)

Lyrics on pages 20–21: "First in My Heart" by Kelly Minter © 2007 ThankYou Music.

Some excerpts taken from: The Living Room Series: *No Other Gods: Confronting Modern Day Idols*
© 2007 Kelly Minter (Nashville: LifeWay Christian Resources).

LCCN 2008920367
ISBN 978-0-7814-4897-0
eISBN 978-1-4347-0294-4

© 2008 Kelly Minter

The Team: Andrea Christian, Karen Lee-Thorp, Theresa With, Jack Campbell, and Karen Athen
Cover/Interior Design: The Visual Republic, Alexis Goodman
Cover Photos: © fStop Photography/Veer; © DigitalVision/Getty Images; Jacky Simanzik, Photocase.com

Printed in the United States of America
First Edition 2008

10 11 12 13 14

092713

# CONTENTS

# 1

## THE FRIST

There's a certain theme in my life, one that continues to cycle around no matter how old or "wise" I become. It's one of those lifelong lessons I've never fully mastered, the kind that God will not recant on, a lesson he's not afraid to deliver to me over and over again in different packaging: Oh wow, it's … you again.

I don't know if you have one of these, that running area of life that seems to be the target of every sermon, Scripture, and circumstance. It's an area of growth you can't seem to get away from, the one that God is always prodding and pruning even at the most inconvenient of times, like holidays. Can I not just eat my turkey without my character being refined? It's a phenomenon, but God doesn't even take Thanksgiving off, except perhaps in the rest of the world where they don't celebrate it.

Never does he slumber; he is always working on this recycling theme: No gods before God. It's the first of the Ten Commandments and one of the most fundamental tenets of the Christian faith. How hard can this be? Yet just as I think I have a handle on it, another false god is exposed in my life. And I'm not talking about a physical statue that I accidentally stumble upon in the recesses of my closet, or a stone idol that I occasionally pray to. Nothing like that. But … sort of like that.

o   o   o

The other day I coerced one of my self-employed friends, Alli, to justify my neglect of work by heading with me to the Frist Museum in the middle of the day. It's essential to take others down with you when playing hooky—there are certain delinquent behaviors that must be done in groups. Fortunately Alli was an easy sell, since she's far more hip than I am and holds a season pass. With a mere phone call, work was tabled and we were off to Egypt—at least to the bits they could fit in the Frist.

We followed each other around with headsets and MP3 players that gave us the history of each piece. I kept making Alli pause her machine so I could comment, as if I had something to add to the British historian eloquently whispering in our ears. There were all sorts of wild displays, from standard mummies to children's games whose stakes were a little higher than I was comfortable with—eternal damnation for the loser. Hadn't they heard of Candyland? We saw ornate jewelry, fine paintings, and a tiny wooden chair over two thousand years old. It intrigued me to think of all the history that little chair had made it through—the crumbling of massive empires, the birth of Christ, and I'm guessing a lot of family squabbles. I'm sure it was very tired of being sat on. I can't remember our favorite exhibit, though I do recall us tarrying over a mummified cat that looked strangely like a hot dog. Not something I would have tried to preserve, but that's just me.

Even beyond the disturbing animal mummies, I have a poignant memory that I will never forget. It was one of the first things Alli and I saw upon entering the exhibit, and it was the last thing I remembered: a towering statue in the form of a sphinx with human legs holding out a symbol of life. The colossus was a bit cracked in places and a few pieces from the face had broken off, but for the most part it had fared well. The British voice in my headset said that the Egyptians would bow down before this exact statue hoping that life would be extended to them.

As I took notice of every detail, I remember thinking how I couldn't imagine that anyone would ever believe that this lifeless rock could do anything, much less give life. I remember thinking how strange it hit me, how I could never see myself hoping for life to spring from stone. Until the next words that crossed through my mind were *You do it all the time.* (This was no longer the British woman.) In fact, the words weren't even audible, but every bit as definitive. If you can know a silent voice, I knew this one.

*Lord, I would never look for life from something like this.*

*But you look for life in lesser things than me all the time, every day.*

I was struck. Quiet, I stood before this idol suddenly aware that all the things I had placed my full hope in were not a hair more able. Suddenly I realized that I had been looking to weak things, even *good* things, for life that only Christ can give. If I could display the images that splashed through my mind, you would have seen the statue turn into familiar faces from my life, career paths, and dreams. Not necessarily bad things, just things that had become detrimental because I had exalted them as gods, things I believed could bring me life.

As I continued staring, I thought about the idols of our culture: the television, body image, boyfriends, girlfriends, food, shopping, family, children, alcohol, money, houses, spouses, drugs, religion, even our own sense of righteousness. Ouch. The cracked rock statue didn't seem so silly after all. In fact, if only the ancient Egyptians could see us today: an extra helping of cookie-dough ice cream. A one-night stand. Hours of meaningless sitcoms. A bottle of vodka. They would probably shake their heads in bewilderment, wondering what any of these things held over their sleek stone images.

As the Lord continued to expose all the things I had put in place of him, I realized that this was not unique to me. Passages from Genesis and Isaiah, Proverbs and Ecclesiastes, the Psalms and the Gospels, Ruth, Romans, 1 John, and virtually every other book in the Bible address the issue of false gods in one way or another. It is a ubiquitous theme. The problem is, when we come across these passages, we often think of statues, sculpted idols, and foreign countries. The entire concept is relegated to far-off peoples in far-off lands. We don't think of the litany of modern-day gods we depend on daily for comfort, relief, protection, happiness, life.…

Or, if we do think of these things, we tend to think of the ones that are on the universally "bad" list: sexual sins, pornography, alcoholism, and drug addiction. But what about the false gods that are inherently good? Things like friends, spouses, material possessions? The things that have only become bad because we have made them the "ultimate" things in our lives. In some ways, this feels far more common. John Calvin put it similarly: "The evil in our desire typically does not lie in what we want, but that we want it too much."[1]

Ah, yes. I have wanted some darn good things a bit too much a time or two. Good things that became ultimate things that became controlling things. Things I bowed down to, perhaps not literally, but with every other piece of my being. Not too different from the Egyptians. After all, they bowed for the same reason we do: a desire for life.

As I walked away from the Frist that day, I was thankful for the unexpected but freeing moment that caused me to further relish the voice of the Holy Spirit. It wasn't condemning but enlightening, gentle but convicting. A conviction that demanded my repentance while extending the truth that God wanted me to trust him for far more. To clear out the idols in my life, not for the sake of legalism but for a much grander purpose: to make room for the God of gods to dwell. To see him do more than I could ask or think—more than a rock statue or a husband or a martini could ever provide.

Perhaps you are longing for the same things. Exhausted by the strong cords of a small god. Weary from serving something that forever promises but never delivers. Angry at an idol that constantly leaves you disappointed, but swears there is no other place to go. If only the Egyptians had known there was a God stronger than the stone sphinx. If only we knew. I talked Alli's ear off about it on the way home. I think she was really missing the British lady.

# 2

# GOD AND GODS

My moment at the Frist was a milestone for me, an Ebenezer of sorts in the middle of an already focused journey I had been taking on the topic of false gods. I had spent the previous year researching the subject for a Bible study curriculum I was writing, and the years before living out my own research as God had dealt with me profoundly on more idols I could feign excitement over. My own journey brings chapter 2 of the book of Hosea to mind—the passage where God relentlessly pursues Israel and Hosea relentlessly pursues his wayward wife, Gomer, while both Israel and Gomer chase other lovers. The Lord hedges in his straying bride, thwarting her every move and wooing her into the desert so that he can speak tenderly to her. That had been my life—lots of desert minutiae.

I was just beginning to see what might be rooftops and charming streets and smokestacks in the distance—signs that the Lord was indeed leading me out of the desert. (And by the way, if you happen to find yourself in such a season of trial or discipline, may I offer Psalm 126:5 as a breath of hope: "Those who sow in tears will reap with songs of joy.")

As the Lord faithfully turned my valley of trouble into a door of hope (Hos. 2:15), some people I greatly admired asked me to write a Bible study, but at first the subject matter remained unclear. I knew the message needed to percolate until I could move with clarity, so I invited four girls over for Mexican and discussion to begin an eight-week Bible study with no set theme that ended up lasting a year and a half. (I found you can get a lot out of people when salsa is involved.) After cooking for about the third time in my life—kudos to my friends for coming back—we sat in my living room, brainstorming for a yet-to-be Bible study curriculum, uncertain where it was all going but praying it was divinely directed.

We made ourselves comfortable and conversed about most anything you could think of: identity, purpose, body image, wanting something "more" in life, singleness, marital strains, church, identity, our relevance as individuals. I scribbled on typing paper with a Sharpie, circling the poignant thoughts, hoping all this would lead to a cohesive topic of study. I never imagined our streams of consciousness would take us to something as seemingly dated as false gods, but by night's end our musings had led us exactly there—it's just that I still couldn't quite see it.

The next morning I nestled into one of my favorite chairs, balancing my tea on the armrest—a precarious move over my cream rug—with my Bible on my lap. I was reading through the Bible in a year, and it happened that I was in 2 Kings 17, which wouldn't have been so out of the ordinary, except for verse 33 that arrested my attention: "They worshiped the LORD, but they also served their own gods." Verse 41 further compounded the description: "Even while these people were worshiping the LORD, they were serving their idols." God and gods: Both were occupying space in their jewelry boxes of time, heart, and service. The people were living split lives, worshipping the One while serving the others.

As I pondered this concept, my mind reeled back to the previous night's discussion with the girls, one that had been full of questions and longings about what it means to live as Christians in relevant and meaningful ways, what living in freedom with purpose and identity actually looks like. Yet somehow the incredibly simplistic phrases in 2 Kings melted the trivial details that surrounded our wonderings. The vagueness of our striving and frustration had been sharpened to a point: We all claimed God as our God, but we had been serving lesser things.

Could it be that we were indebted to other gods, though we sat in the front row at church and served the coffee? We claimed the Bible as our source of truth, but were our real counselors coming from movie screens and magazines? Perhaps so many of our struggles—lack of freedom, loss of spiritual desire, slavery to image, perfectionism, confusion, and the list is infinite—had much to do with this idea of God *and*.… The people in 2 Kings were worshipping God, but they were also serving their idols.

Both verses speak of worship to God but service to idols. I believe there is an exquisite distinction between the two words. For so much of my life I worshipped God: showing up for church, singing hymns, helping in the nursery, reading my Bible, confessing my belief in him. Yet if you could have witnessed what I was controlled by, what motivated and moved me, you would have seen that in many cases it was not God at all, but my idols. Not carved images, but people, career paths, materialism, acceptance, and more.

God was getting my worship on some level, but my gods were getting my service.

o   o   o

I grew up in a Christian home in a fairly "Christian" society, and I think this contradiction of worship to God and service to idols permeates the Christian community I've experienced. Just this morning a group of college girls gathered at my house for breakfast and study to discuss this very issue. A few of the girls expressed the interesting notion that idols were such a part of their daily lives that they had consented to the idea that "this is just the way it is." I thought this was a poignant expression of honesty and vulnerability, because who hasn't succumbed to such a thought? We walk such a compartmentalized line of church on Sunday and an occasional Bible study if we're extra serious, all the while relying on our friends, boyfriends, spouses, careers, outward beauty, and skill to truly carry us along. It's rare that we come across someone who has broken the mold, one who truly lives—albeit imperfectly—with God as the driving force and love of their life. So many of us claim and worship God, but we've come to accept a lifestyle that depends upon most everything else. And whatever we depend upon we will most definitely serve.

When we try to house both God and gods, we are left with half-hearted living. It is painfully ungratifying. And I believe it's possibly one of the reasons why so many of us—including me—have been stuck. Basically, we have edged God out. We have left him with little room in our hearts. Our false gods have taken up our most treasured spaces; we leave God no place to show himself strong on our behalf.

After I pondered these things further, I realized that 2 Kings 17:33 was the seed our study was to grow out of. It was why the Lord had tenderly led me into the desert for such a long season, so that at the end of my journey I could have the same exchange with God that the Israelites had with him in Hosea 2:23: "I will say ... 'You are my people'; and they will say, 'You are my God.'" Though I will never fully rid myself of false gods in this lifetime, I emerged from my desert trials knowing that God was indeed mine and that I wanted him more than any lesser, entangling idol.

This conclusion came at a heart level, the place where our false gods are constructed. It required a lot of my time and attention, since there is much to discover about them: What do modern-day idols look like? How do we make them? How do we destroy them? In what ways do they affect us? Which ones are we serving? Why are we serving them? These are the questions this book attempts to explore.

And yet our foray into such heart work must go beyond the dangerous place of turning from something without turning to Someone, which is much like the parable of the man who sent an evil spirit out of his house, cleaned and swept, only for the demon to return with seven more. The man's final condition ended up worse than the first (Luke 11:24–26). It is my supreme desire for us to discover not only the process of turning from our idols, but also the freedom of turning to the true God in all of his glory. We make room in our hearts so Christ can dwell—it's the upside to all this idol talk, and it's the remedy to some of our heartache, entanglement, and disappointment.

Somewhere in the middle of this entire discovery I wrote a song called "First in My Heart." It's a prayer of sorts, perhaps one you can offer up for yourself as you seek to find God as, well, God. He is worth whatever pains you may take in the journey.

"First in My Heart"

So this is love, it feels like war
To slay my gods by the sword
Making room for you to dwell
Here inside of me unrivaled
Though it cost me everything
Only you will be

First in my heart, first in my mind
And in everything I long for in this life
First in my dreams, first in my eyes
Before every other love that I desire

So settle in and you never mind
These trembling hands, these teary eyes
Cause I never knew it'd hurt so bad
To turn my back upon this golden calf
Let its memory fade away
Till you alone remain

> First in my heart, first in my mind
> And in everything I long for in this life
> First in my dreams, first in my eyes
> Before every other love that I desire

Take these idols a million miles
From the allegiance of my soul
Still this hunger with your wonder
Till only you will … only, only, only you will be

> First in my heart, first in my mind
> And in everything I long for in this life
> First in my dreams, first in my eyes
> Before every other love that I desire

*To do your own study on the topic of this book, check out the Bible study: *No Other Gods: Confronting Our Modern Day Idols*, which is the first release of The Living Room Series (LifeWay Church Resources), www.lifeway.com/livingroomseries.

# 3

# SUNDAY SCHOOL

I remember when I was small, sitting in Sunday school and hearing about the false gods from ancient biblical times. We were blessed with some high-tech, er, flannelgraph renderings of these distant idols. Smoothing them onto the staticky board passed the time until the most meaningful part of the morning rolled around: graham crackers and apple juice. Fig Newtons were swapped in on special occasions—oh, for the good life.

On the best days we'd have Mrs. Seager read to us from colorfully illustrated books about late missionaries from foreign lands. We'd learn about the witch doctors in the villages and the special animals the tribes set apart to worship. Sometimes we'd even get to see real-life slides of people with grass skirts, and elephant tusks drilled into their noses, raising their hands while chanting to the gods of the sky. This was some good stuff, every bit as thrilling as any Saturday-morning kid show, and particularly appealing to childlike wanderlust.

The missionary slides provided a lens into diverse cultures that not only seemed distant but altogether fairy-tale. Where I grew up on 12718 Carlsbad Court—"real life," that is—we never saw anything like this. Everyone I knew believed in the Christian God, the God of the Bible—hello, who else was there? I mean, except for those other false gods that I learned about in Sunday school, the ones where the people who worshipped them dressed and talked funny. I don't for a moment regret that exposure and in fact am the richer for it, but at the time I couldn't assimilate the idea of idols into anything modern. They certainly didn't have anything to do with my normal life. For me, the concept was land- and time-locked in remote jungles.

o   o   o

It wasn't until many years later that the notion of false gods began to thaw for me, its reality trickling into unexpected parts of my life. I had become lassoed by people I wanted approval from, occasionally throwing out my values and beliefs at the feet of their acceptance. I'd become trapped on the ladder of achievement, each rung only as good as getting to the next. I was ruled by my selfishness and dragged around by cavernous desires. Although I was a Christian, so many other things led the way besides God. I professed God, but, functionally, I allowed a slew of other things to act as him.

I came to experientially understand something that Ken Sande put this way: "An idol is not simply a statue of wood, stone, or metal; it is anything we love and pursue in place of God, and can also be referred to as a 'false god' or a 'functional god.' In biblical terms, an idol is something other than God that we set our hearts on (Luke 12:29; 1 Cor. 10:6), that motivates us (1 Cor. 4:5), that masters or rules us (Ps. 119:133), or that we serve (Matt. 6:24)."[2]

Who knew I had so much in common with the exquisite and exotic natives I used to peer in on as a kid? Their god-forms were different, but their function the same: What they might get out of a good chant to the sun god, I might find at the mall in a pair of jeans. If their culture pushed women to be one of fifty-two wives for a satisfying image, ours promoted more sophisticated methods like bar hopping and one-night stands. It's the "anything we love and pursue in place of God" part that universally connects our Western world with not only the foreign countries I used to learn about as a kid, but the biblical cultures as well. When it comes to what we set our hearts on—what masters or motivates us other than God—this issue of idolatry is as present and relevant as anything we can hold in our hand.

The term *functional god* has become most helpful to me because it pulls the concept of idolatry out of distant lands and times, out of the Frist Museum, and places it into modern, real life—places like Carlsbad Court. Suddenly, it's not just about who I proclaim is my God, but who actually functions as him. I can say that I believe in the God of the Bible, I can profess Christ as Savior and even serve the coffee at Sunday school, but who or what functions as my God in the moments of tragedy, celebration, or walking the aisles of the grocery store can be an entirely different matter.

o   o   o

When I nestle into my covers at night and my thoughts begin to twirl with worry or sadness, to whom or what do I turn? If only this person would understand what I need in life and deliver it, perhaps I would be content. If only I had a husband to hold me. If I could just get to the next plane of my career. If I made more money and could travel in decadence. If I had children to love and appreciate me—then I would be fulfilled. I suppose I'll flip channels and get my mind on something else. Too often we profess God but look to everything else to function as him. Even perfectly good things. Things that in and of themselves are pure and right and gifts from God but have become a problem simply because of the placement they have in our lives.

Richard Keyes puts it this way:

> An idol is something within creation that is inflated to function as God. All sorts of things are potential idols, depending only on our attitudes and actions toward them.... Idolatry may not involve explicit denials of God's existence or character. It may well come in the form of an over-attachment to something that is, in itself, perfectly good.... An idol can be a physical object, a property, a person, an activity, a

role, an institution, a hope, an image, an idea, a pleasure, a hero—anything that can substitute for God.[3]

I love Keyes' definition, cause it's essential to move away from the notion that a false god is only made up of something inherently bad. Again, there are the obvious ones like drugs, excessive alcohol, immorality, but an idol can also be an unexpected thing like a new house, career, husband, child, friend—anything that we are inordinately attached to. Tim Keller, pastor of Redeemer Presbyterian Church in New York City, poignantly says, "Idolatry is attached to everything. All of our bitterness, all our impurity, all our malice, all of our problems, everything that troubles us is a result of idolatry. And what is idolatry? It's taking a good thing and making it an ultimate thing."

My legalistic nature loves to piously pat itself on the back as it looks down on all those poor souls who are trapped by the big, bad sin idols. The ones that none of the rest of us struggle with, the ones that make us feel so much better because we don't. But neither Keyes' nor Keller's definition allows for such self-righteousness, because idolatry is not just about an affair, a drug addiction, or a stone statue, but is anything—even something inherently good—that we have turned into an ultimate thing in our lives.

James 4:2 further expounds on this concept. The *Holman Christian Standard Bible* reads, "You desire and do not have. You murder and covet and cannot obtain." The word *desire* (or *crave* or *lust*) is taken from the Greek word *epithumio*, which literally means "to set the heart upon, i.e. long for (rightfully or otherwise)—covet, desire, would fain, lust after."[4] This is key to more fully understanding what James is saying. He says the cravings that often cause us pain or get us into trouble are not necessarily cravings for wrong or evil things. I have read the book of James so many times, and every time I've gotten to 4:1–2, I have conjured up all the desires I've had for bad things, convinced that those were the problem. It never occurred to me that my desires for right things could turn excessive and disproportionate and cause the great pain and unrest that James describes. It's the unsuspected good things that have most often tripped me up.

o   o   o

I asked my friend Scott if he wanted to run with me the other day, hoping that his presence would ensure my actually doing it. (Intentions can be so misleading.) He kindly obliged, which meant he had to cut his gait in half, which meant he was basically walking, which meant he was babysitting me while I ran. The one thing he was sure to get out of it, though, was some good conversation, as I can chat it up with the best of them. My friend Margaret used to invite me along on her runs by calling me up and asking if AM radio was available—apparently I can cover a broad range of useless subjects. The attraction is that it's sort of like running with a noise machine, I think.

I don't remember where Scott and I were in conversation when I began plummeting unannounced toward the asphalt. It's true what people say about instantaneous catastrophes happening in slow motion, though I think it's the person who actually slows down, counting every millisecond as a vital decision-making opportunity. Right before I hit the ground, body flailing almost parallel to the street, I tried to thrust my right foot back underneath me but couldn't get it far enough forward to accomplish any kind of save. Since Plan A failed and time was thin, I reverted to the old standby of casting both hands out in front of me—the standby that spares your body but almost always ends up breaking your wrists. As I braced for impact, I entered that precise point where slow motion suddenly turns real time, and everything you were desperately trying to avoid during those 0.8 seconds happens anyway.

I shamelessly writhed on the pavement, knees and hands throbbing and bleeding. I rolled around like you do in those situations, moaning and throwing out non-words. I was in such pain, but my dignity cried louder for a reason behind my downfall. I peeled my head from the pavement and craned my neck just enough to make out what might have been the culprit. Surely I hadn't tripped over my own feet, although this wasn't impossible for my pigeon-toed frame. There on the horizon, peeking out of an otherwise level street, stood a proud and unfaltering nail. It's amazing the things you see while on the same plane as something.

"Are you okay? Let me help you up!"

"I just need to lay here for a minute," I gasped. "I think it was that nail back there." Scott went a few feet back and pried my bitter nemesis out of the street.

A few people who were out on evening strolls with their dogs inquired from across the way, "Can we help? Is everything okay?" As if to protect my dignity, Scott held the nail up to the neighborhood, very Statue of Liberty–like, and yelled, "It was this naaaiiiilllll!" He rightly understood that it was far more important for people to know why I fell, as opposed to whether or not I was going to live. After a few awkward minutes, Scott—doing a great job of running-babysitter—extended his hand and helped me up. No broken bones, just a little blood and a few bruises that looked like fairly impressive modern art on my knees.

As I limped off, I noticed Scott dropping the nail into his pocket with a sinister expression. He insisted it would one day show up at the most unexpected time. I reminded him that as clever as he was, it had shown up unexpectedly the first time. I was not much interested in see- ing it again, though I suspect I'll probably unwrap it one day at one of those ridiculous white elephant Christmas parties. Or perhaps Scott is hanging onto it for the metaphorical purpose of reminding me how easily I can be tripped up in life. He's the most generous and kind man you'll ever meet, but this is not beneath him.

o   o   o

As I run, walk, and at times hobble through life, I wish it were just the flesh and bones of my knees and hands that were vulnerable to such snares. Though I have a little scar on my left hand to remind me of the day the tip of my shoe hooked the tip of a nail—slamming my body to the ground—I have heart scars and soul contusions that have come from unexpected places, places where I had given myself to idols, and not just the crazy bad ones, but the good ones that had become bad, simply because, as John Calvin put it, I desired them too much.

Psalm 106:36 says, "They worshiped their idols, which became a snare to them." My personal version adds, "... which became an invisible nail sticking out of an otherwise smooth surface while you were pleasantly minding your own business." Or something like that. I was intrigued by one of the definitions for *snare*, which describes the word as a situation that is both alluring and dangerous. The idols—both good and bad objects of my desire—have been equally seductive and harmful, which is what I'm afraid makes them so deceiving.

No longer is a false god just an esoteric concept from foreign countries and Bible times, no longer a merely sinful object that I'm supposed to keep my distance from. Instead, it's whatever steals my heart's affection from God, and whatever inordinately motivates me. Simply put, it's anything and everything that takes the place of God in my life. If only I could have grasped this from the colorful, missionary books—although I'm pretty sure it still would have taken a good nail.

# 4

# BACK PAIN

"You shall have no other gods before me."

I grew up with the Ten Commandments—reading them, memorizing them, singing about them: "Number one, we've just begun, God should be first in your life! Number two, the idol rule, those graven images … aren't nice." (It's a catchy little number, that Ten Commandments song.) Oh my, the things that stick in my brain for decades, while where I put my keys ten minutes ago is pure mystery.

As I grow older, I become more convinced of the need to revisit certain things learned in childhood so I can experience them freshly. To encounter the seemingly antiquated and discover it anew. Especially if some of those things are biblical or doctrinal things that have lost their meaning for me. However, if perhaps you grew up not singing and dancing to the Ten Commandments, I'm pretty sure it just means you have less to overcome, fewer counseling bills and stuff.

I love Scripture so much and have found the Spirit behind its words to be life's marrow. It has instructed, comforted, grounded, and guided me through desperate as well as celebratory times. Even Old Testament passages like the Ten Commandments—which are getting increasingly poor PR these days—I've found practical and freeing. (The bad PR might be due in part to some off-centered fundamentalists who have somehow become synonymous with these commands.)

Regardless, Exodus 20 gives us far more than an out-of-touch list or a grouping of religious suggestions. Yet placed up against the whole of Scripture, we find that they are far less than what is needed to transform the heart—we learn from the failings of the Israelites in the Old Testament and from the Epistles in the New Testament that we can't keep them on our own. That only Jesus Christ can fulfill such laws, and that he did so on our behalf. It is the great mystery of Christ in us, the hope of glory! This is important to understand, even in the slightest manner, so we don't go zealously running off to have no other gods before us with our own self-righteousness as the fuel behind our venture. We must have Christ to work this out in us, but a little more on this later.

When looking at the Ten Commandments, apart from the kiddo melody in my head, I must take note of the order, the first being, "I am the LORD your God." Here he sets up his godhead, which is essential, because if we don't have this piece settled, the following nine commands become pretty arbitrary: If someone else is God, then whatever further commands he has are irrelevant. So the Lord begins with what really must be the first rule, which is that he is God.

o o o

First Timothy 1:17 says, "Now to the King eternal, immortal, invisible, the only God, be honor and glory for ever and ever. Amen." I imagine that this is not unique to my generation or culture, but the truth of one singular God is becoming increasingly fuzzy and vague. It's far more acceptable to consider other religions with other gods as perfectly reasonable, sort of like what's good for you is good with me, and if in fact you believe otherwise, you are viewed as intolerant, which is one of the worst things you can be viewed as today.

Open-mindedness is celebrated as the ultimate virtue, though it's imperative to note that the only time you can't be open-minded is if you're open to the possibility of there being only one God with one gospel. That would be closed-mindedness, even though being open-minded inherently means that you are closed to the idea of one God with one way. And if the truth really is that there is only one God, what a tremendous disservice it is, not only to God but to those around us, to casually accept or promote what is false in the name of open-mindedness or tolerance. I'm all about both of these concepts and indeed strive for them, but not at the expense of truth.

o o o

The focus of this book isn't so much about the idea of the existence of only one God as it relates to the gods of other religions, but as it relates to all the functional gods we depend upon in our lives. However, our aim is lost if this first point is not settled that there is only one God. It is so essential that the only true and wise God be exalted, not only above all religious gods but over all the things we put in place of him: people, material possessions, chemicals, spouses, work.... But in order to get there, we must first resolve that there stands but one Savior, one Spirit, and one Father, who mysteriously make up the essence of one God.

Naturally following the first command, "I am the LORD your God," comes the second, which is to have no other gods before him. I would like to think that since God is God, having false gods before him would be the one thing that could go without saying. Yet instead of keeping silent, we experience him spelling it out for the Israelites in noteworthy detail. "You shall not make for yourself an idol in the form of anything in heaven above or on the earth beneath or in the waters below." This rules out the defiant little piece of my brain that wonders if, say, in the fourth dimension, on an unknown planet, outside of the time continuum, would it maybe be okay for a teeny, tiny idol to exist there? But alas, God covers the entire universe, even the water beneath the earth, which I didn't even know existed. He really leaves us no wiggle room here, which I find a little humorous because he knows our frame and our tendency toward loopholes so well that he must rule out every conceivable place for a false god to exist.

I grew up across the street from a brother and sister named Josh and Sunshine (her real name), and this was way before people started naming their kids things like Apple and Cocoa—their family was pretty ahead of their time. Anyhow, Josh was this real bundle of creative and spontaneous energy, which was tons of fun to watch from across the street, but not as enjoyable for his parents, I presume. Sunshine and I were the same age, and Josh a bit younger, so by the time we were preteens we got to babysit him on occasion for large sums of change—approximately fifty cents an hour split between the two of us. I so wish I'd known about compounding interest then.

One day his parents had to dash out before Sunshine and I were home from school, leaving about a forty-five-minute overlap of home-alone time for Josh. His parents sat him down and went over every rule they could conceive of: no walking to the store, no horseplaying, no erroneous phone-calling, no crazy tricks with the dog…. I don't know what in the world was wrong with them, but they left out no climbing the neighbor's tree and using it as a launching pad from which to spring onto their roof … which is exactly where Sunshine and I found Josh playing when we got home. When confronted by his parents, he accurately and innocently defended himself: "You never told me I wasn't allowed on the Masons' roof."

And so for the Josh in all of us, God puts the entire universe out of play for false gods—even the really fun roof next door.

While still addressing the second command, the Lord continues: "You shall not bow down to them or worship them; for I, the LORD your God, am a jealous God." So, even if there happened to be an idol lying around that the Israelites didn't create, there could be no bowing down or serving it. I think God put so much detail into this because he knows our propensity to worship what is not him, and he understands the frailty in us that leans toward what is false as opposed to falling before what is real. He knows we will make gods out of anything we can get our hands on, from statues, to planets, to people, to pizza.

This is why he had to set the order. To begin by stating the essence of his being: God. To continue by instructing that, because he is indeed God, nothing and no one else can go before him.

o   o   o

Last week I spent a few consecutive days on my back. I still don't know exactly what went wrong, but somehow I twisted it about as awkwardly as you can wrench a back without being a clay toy. It started with a little tightness in my lower back after a short run, followed by more stiffness after the next day's jog. By the following morning, my back had seized up, which wouldn't have been so bad except that it froze at around a thirty-degree angle. I was in such pain I could hardly breathe, so I called my friend April, who in *Anne of Green Gables* terminology is my "kindred spirit."

After opening the door and taking one look at me, April cupped her hand over her mouth and in a supportive and purely non-self-centered tone said, "I'm going to vomit." I admit my posture was a little bizarre, but it wasn't like I was gushing blood—just a little bent.

"Well please don't, 'cause I can't bend down to clean it up."

"Seriously, Kelly, stand up straight," she implored. (April implores me a lot. She's even starting to use the word *beseech*, as in, "I beseech you not to pick anything up while you're like this.")

"Please don't make me call second-tier friends," I pleaded at an angle.

April's exceptionally competent, so once she got over my unnatural posture she brought me ice, made me call the doctor, and scrounged up some heavy-duty Motrin worth illegal amounts of milligrams, judging by their size. The next day she drove me to the chiropractor and sat in the waiting room for two hours, which more than made up for her initial squeamishness. I hobbled around the corner into the doctor's office, who incidentally was young, single, and shockingly handsome—of Hollywood proportions. It was yet another reminder that you can never let your makeup guard down. Just when you think it's safe to leave the house with greasy hair, in sweatpants, no makeup, and at a significantly unattractive tilt—*bam*—you get the Brad Pitt of the chiropractic world.

After he ran some preliminary tests and checked my X-rays, he concluded that my facet joints had significantly stiffened, causing my muscles to spasm in reaction to the injury. He explained that when a person's facet joints freeze up, the muscles go into a protective, tightening mode so nothing can hurt the joints further, thus causing my twisted position. For some reason this made him send me to a woman across the hall who said she was going to "adjust" me. I found out that this really isn't the right word for such a procedure. *Adjust* is entirely too benign a word to describe what happened to me—it was more like trickery, followed by violent jerking.

Before the "adjustment," I am not exaggerating when I tell you that I was in such acute pain it took me a couple of minutes just to figure out a way onto the table. I would have been hesitant for a feather to have landed on my back—much more someone applying premeditated force. After I made it onto the table, the woman pulled my arms and legs into a pretzel-like contortion, which was surprisingly accomplished without pain. She then began to slowly roll my body back and forth in smooth and gentle motions, conversing with me as she went. And I am definitely not sprucing up the truth when I tell you that simply out of nowhere—just plain, out of the blue— she thrust herself into my leg, in what felt like cracking my spine in half. I yelled, as if I were going to have to fight her off of me, like this was malpractice at its dirtiest. What was wrong with this woman?

I thought about screaming for Mr. Movie Star across the way to come save me, but refrained when I realized that all this body slamming was perhaps part of the plan (it also could've definitely ruined any chance of dinner and a movie). The only problem was that she wanted to then do the same thing on my other side. It's like someone suddenly punching you in the ear, and then telling you to hold still and relax while they do it to the other one. Not for the fainthearted.

After my foray into the world of "adjustments," I was sent to yet another room where they do interferentials and ultrasound to loosen the muscles that are inflamed because they just snapped you in half. They hurt you then heal you, which is a brilliant business concept if nothing else. A couple hours later I left the offices feeling surprisingly looser. Who knew such aggressive tactics could be so successful?

With each successive visit to the chiropractor, my posture continued to improve (though I attribute this to the cute doctor and not so much to the adjuster lady). It reminded me of how dependent I am upon the core of my body being stable and mobile. If any piece slips out of place, even so much as a centimeter, things like bending down or reaching for a piece of chocolate become dramatic feats. Nothing works if the spine is not where it should be. It's just the order of the body.

And so it is with this fundamental piece of God being God, and God being the only God. When this gets out of whack in our belief system, the entire structure falls apart, the chain reaction affecting things you wouldn't imagine. It's like trying to run or reach or bend with a bad back. It's painful, and eventually impossible. If God is not God, if he is not the only God in our lives, then his commands and principles and truths become matters of suggestion that we're free to savor or toss at our whims.

o    o    o

We all have different stories and circumstances in the wake of where we currently tread just like the variety of Israelites who stood before the Lord while he gave them his commands. You may be unsure about whether or not the God of the Bible is the only God. You haven't settled his position in your mind as it relates to other religions and other gods. Or you may emphatically claim that he is the only God from a faith standpoint but have other personal, functional gods that you lean upon for daily life. I have experienced this latter situation at many seasons, which I hope are becoming fewer, and have found them unsatisfying and unstable.

But regardless of where you are on the spectrum, the Lord cannot stress enough how essential, how vital it is to settle this one truth in your mind: his godhead. This is the core by which everything else moves and breathes. And if you want to get there, but you're a little stuck and just aren't quite convinced, genuinely cry out to him for his voice. He can assure you, not because he has to prove himself, but because he loves us and gave his life for us. As Paul says in 1 Timothy 2:4, God "wants all men to be saved and to come to a knowledge of the truth."

If you need help in thinking this issue through, there's a wealth of good books that explain why God is God.[5] Talking to a mature Christian friend—somebody who isn't threatened by real questions and honest doubts—is also hugely helpful.

The truth of God being God is as fundamental as the spine. His supremacy and singularity as God are essential to our going any further in the conquest of our idols. If we are unsure of this point, if we believe that many gods do in fact exist, then truly there can be no idols in the traditional sense. Put more simply, false gods only exist if there is one true God put up against them. If this goes away, then everything is free game and the idea of scrutinizing the place of idols in our lives becomes a meaningless exercise. But according to the Bible, polytheism (many gods) is unacceptable, not because the truth of God is close-minded or dated or intolerant, but for beautifully counter-reasoning: because God seeks to save, reaching the ends of the earth, every nation, tribe, and tongue, with his gospel, with what James 1:25 refers to as the perfect law of liberty, the law of loving the one true God.

And to partake of such refreshing liberty we must go a step beyond merely approaching God as God, but as *our* God. Knowing the real God is remarkably personal, which I find a bit scary at times, yet breathtakingly intimate. A personal invitation for relationship awaits....

# 5

# YOUR GOD

"I am the LORD your God." It is the core of our beliefs, the essential resolve from which Christianity stems. Without this fundamental starting point—the Lord is God—our belief system loses its backbone. If he is not actually God, or if what he proclaims is not truth, we have nothing on which to stand. Yet this opening line of the Ten Commandments serves as more than just a proclamation of God's deity, as that could be said as "I am the Lord God." But an additional word is written, one that takes his unattainable God-ness and endearingly personalizes it, making it "I am the LORD *your* God." It's the one word that changes everything, the word that brings what could have been a faceless God into a reachable One, the word that sparks the question, "Is he God, or is he your God?" And if he is God, but not your God, I would like to propose that it's a relationship not strong enough to keep you from false gods.

This personal element is so essential because it's the fundamental nature of how God created us. He intended us to be in relationship with him, this not being a special cherry on top that only certain people get if they're really lucky. If we're not in personal relationship with him, we will absolutely be in it with something else, a false god, because our hearts are designed in such a way as to be intimate with something. John H. Sailhamer, scholar and professor, says in his book *The Pentateuch as Narrative,* "He is a personal God and will not be satisfied with anything less than a personal relationship with men and women whom he created in His image."[6]

This is significant to me, because I think so much of my growing up I took the "He is God" view—which is better than "He is not God" but is dramatically lacking compared to "He is your God." Although I believed in him for eternal life, for his Spirit to indwell me, and for forgiveness of sin, the really intimate "your" piece was missing. Actually, from my perspective, the "my" piece was lacking; he was oh-so-very-much God, but I had little experience with him being my God, making for an anemic relationship.

I feared him and wanted to do what he said, cause as a little kid I wasn't so thrilled about prospects like judgment and wrath. I figured it was a good idea to toe the line and keep the rules, but you can do this for only so long for someone who isn't really yours. Eventually I got frustrated and burnt out, because only in relationship can God's laws be walked out. They are so unnatural for one thing, so opposed to what our flesh desires, that keeping them for someone with whom we are not deeply involved becomes a real imposition.

But in order for us to view God as our own, we have to have a story with him. And that story can be three seconds old or forty-six years—there just has to be a little detail written in, something that personalizes the whole thing. So if you just discovered this morning that Jesus Christ died for you and for your grievances against him, that he came to give you freedom and renew your heart, and you find yourself reveling in such glorious redemption—you have a story. You have a God who is not just the Lord God, but who is *your* Lord God, which makes all the difference.

o    o    o

Although I had some precious experiences earlier in life, I began to more deeply understand God as my own while in high school. I started including the specifics of my life in prayer to him, things like asking that my friends Kerry, Emily, and Melanie would come to know him. I prayed for my coaches, that the Holy Spirit inside me would be a blessing and a light to their lives. When deeply hurt by rejection, I shared my tears with the Lord. And after losing my athletic scholarship to college, I learned to trust him as someone deeply involved in my present and future, understanding that my God was not overwhelmed or surprised by what felt like insurmountable trials at the time. As weeks and months passed, I began to recognize his breath coursing through my life, resolving some of the questions while giving me a story that proved yet a little more that he was not only God, but my God.

I think these intimate experiences and the far more profound ones since have caused me to notice something I'd never seen before while reading Exodus 20. I mean, I'd seen it enough to read it, but not enough to know I'd read it. It was a phrase that followed the "I am the LORD your God" introduction but wasn't included in the fun kid song I had learned. After all, when "number six, don't get your kicks from killing one another" is a key line in a song, why would you ever think that something could be missing? And yet, who knew that a pretty significant piece of Scripture didn't get written into the song, or even into the Protestant or Catholic versions of the Ten Commandments for that matter?

I suppose I've never had reason to think about this before, but I recently learned that the Ten Commandments are structured a bit differently from one religion or division to another. It's not that any group has changed what's written in Scripture; it's simply a matter of how they've chosen to divide them and which pieces they've pulled to highlight. The Jews, Protestants, and Catholics emphasize different portions, most of the differences being in the first two commandments. For example, the first commandment in the Catholic version is "I am the LORD your God. You shall have no other gods before me."[7] The first commandment of the Protestants is, "You shall have no other gods but me," followed by their second commandment, "You shall not make unto you any graven images." In essence, the Catholics' first commandment combines what make up commandments one and two for the Protestants.[8]

Because I grew up under the Protestant umbrella, I was aware only of their list, never having any reason to think that other groups organize it differently. (Then again, I was, like, nine when I found out that what I thought was a girl cheese sandwich was actually a grilled cheese one. That finally laid to rest the troubling question of why so many boys shamelessly ate girls' sandwiches.) But here's what the Jews include that no one else does, the part that blessed me so much the other day: "I am the LORD your God, *who brought you out of Egypt, out of the land of slavery.*"

The emphasized portion is the piece that isn't on most of the lists even though it's right there in Scripture. It's not the part people memorize, and I'll admit, it probably doesn't sing as well—harder to rhyme a lot of stuff with "Egypt" or tap your toe to "land of slavery." But these are the stunning and personal qualifications that make the first six words so remarkably endearing. They're the description that make the "your" in "I am the LORD your God" really mean something. It's as if God graciously introduced himself by saying, you all are mine, and by the way, I've done a thing or two to be able to say this.

The Jews obviously embrace this part because it's their heritage. The Israelites suffered in Egypt, were freed through the Red Sea, and were delivered from slavery. Far be it from them not to include those details as part of their Ten Commandments. I suppose the Catholics and Protestants leave this portion out because the detail isn't specific to them, and yet as someone who has teetered on the edge of horrifying precipices, has been a little tied up, miserable in sin, and pretty darn stuck in life, I want to proclaim along with the Israelites that, yes, my God has delivered me, too. My God's arm has raised me out of dreadful waters. My God's mercies have healed some gaping wounds. My God's sovereignty has guided me through blinding valleys. I have a story with the Lord, as the Israelites have a story with him, as you, I pray, have one with him.

o   o   o

Isaiah 46:5, 9 says, "To whom will you compare me or count me equal? To whom will you liken me that we may be compared? … I am God, and there is no other; I am God, and there is none like me." I used to think these verses came off as pious and boastful. But after going round and round with disappointing and destructive idols, I am realizing that these are tender, comforting words that I can hang my life upon. There is no God but God. His sentiments are sweet, but strong. He is not passively requesting our attention. In this passage, he compares himself to gods made from silver and gold that cannot hear the cries of their worshippers. In essence he's saying, who or what do you have that's even remotely like me?

Because God is God, his introduction to the Israelites in Exodus 20 is an exceptionally gracious one. He could have simply stopped at "I am the LORD your God," end of discussion. Or he could have added, "So you'd better do what I say, or shape up, or stop being such jerks running around like turkeys in the desert." He does kind of do this at other times, but not at this moment. The beauty here is that he qualifies his statement by reminding the Israelites of who he's been in their lives and what he's done for them. He shows them that he's not some golden calf off the street proclaiming lordship over them but is the God who has actually engaged in their lives.

To appreciate the weightiness of such a statement, it's helpful to look back in Exodus and see what the Israelites were going through in Egypt and why it was a place of bondage for them. Years before Moses came down from Mount Sinai with the Ten Commandments in his hands, a Hebrew man named Joseph had been sold into Egypt by his brothers. A super-raw deal no doubt, except for the fact that God has this remarkable and miraculous way of taking what people mean for harm and turning it into something good. So even though Joseph had to survive a pit, a prison, and someone else's nagging wife, he eventually ended up second only to Pharaoh in all of Egypt.

Because of an extended famine that lasted seven years, Joseph's entire family migrated to Goshen (northern Egypt) to save their lives. Although the Hebrews and Egyptians wouldn't have necessarily been considered tight pals, this setup worked pretty well for a while, like about as long as the Yankees and Mets could stand one another. It wasn't until Pharaoh and all of Joseph's generation died that problems arose, mostly because the new Pharaoh knew nothing of Joseph, and the Israelites had multiplied so much that he became threatened by their growth. He worried that the Egyptians would get outnumbered and that the Israelites might join their enemies' camp. His solution was to place masters over them whose job it was to oppress them with heavy, forced labor. This went on for about four hundred years (or a little less, depending on what scriptural viewpoint you take).

The slavery and oppression grew fiercer with time, eventually leading to the executions of their baby boys and the addition of insurmountable workloads. Their cries became bitter and hopeless as the severity of their slavery intensified. They didn't have even a flicker of relief, every miserable day bleeding into the next—until God was ready to move, fulfill his covenant, and liberate their lives from such tyranny. The story of how he did this spans several interesting stages, comprised of things like frogs, hail, and water turning to blood. The dramatic story culminates as the Israelites find themselves on the brink of the Red Sea, chariots, hooves, and Egyptians thundering in the background. The Israelites were on their way out, but only if something as impossible as an entire sea decided to split in half—or if God decided to split it and hold it open long enough for all of them to scurry across, then crash it back together at the precise moment the Egyptians reached the center. As long as all this worked out, they were pretty much home free.

We know from the rest of the story that God delivered them in exactly that remarkable way. So when you take into consideration the exceptionally long duration of their suffering and the majestic performance of God's deliverance, suddenly "I am the LORD your God, who brought you out of Egypt, out of the land of slavery" means something profoundly personal. It becomes the beautiful qualification—not that God must qualify himself—of who he is, not just to the Jews but to all who have believed in him.

○   ○   ○

So whether you're an Israelite on the edge of the Red Sea, a wife whose marriage was supernaturally salvaged, an alcoholic who stands brilliantly free, a former sufferer of excruciating depression, or a sinner who's been forgiven, you know him as the Lord your God, who brings you out. This is the sweet extension of relationship that Christianity offers, a story that we are graciously invited into.

And, of course, if you don't yet have a story with him, you most certainly can. Hebrews 12:2 says that Christ is the author and finisher of our faith. He is the author of it, because without him we have no life to be written, and he is the finisher of it, because he has accomplished everything necessary for us to receive forgiveness and salvation. As he hung on the cross and breathed his last breath, he spoke three profoundly simple words: "It is finished." When he died to pay the penalty for our sin, the payment was complete, and it was indeed finished. But mysteriously enough, Christ's finished work is actually the beginning for us, the place where all is paid for, the place where his life can be offered to us so he can not only be God, but our God. And if this truth of a personal saving God is new to you, one of my greatest joys would be for you to know him as such. He is already God regardless of a person's belief or disbelief, but his desire is to be your God, and it's as attainable as trusting him as the only one capable of forgiving you, and therefore saving you from your sin, promising relationship and everlasting life with him. Because we were created for intimacy with our Creator, my prayer is that you find him as your God this sweet hour.

And if you already know him as your personal God, you may be wondering why the pull of such lesser, false gods remains so strong, why you find yourself wrapped up in the tendrils of debilitating idols even though they so painfully pale in comparison to the one true God. Part of the answer to that question lies beneath the surface, requiring a bit of digging for clues as to why it's so easy to fall at the feet of so much less.

# 6

# WHY IDOLS?

If false gods weren't appealing, I suppose we wouldn't seek them out. At the same time, part of their appeal has to do with where we are and where we've come from. What might be attractive to some might not be to others. Certain idols that function "really well" for me wouldn't necessarily tempt another. So much of what draws us to our personal gods has to do with where our needs are, where we hurt, why we hurt, and how we desire that pain to be satiated. It also has to do with our culture and what is promoted to us. In my experience standing in front of the towering stone sphinx, I wasn't moved to worship, mostly because my Western culture hasn't sold that to me. I'd be more tempted by a giant ice-cream cone. Preferably one with peanut-butter chunks.

Though our idols in the West look somewhat different from those in other cultures, no matter their form, the greater our pain and the deeper our wounds, the more vulnerable we are to them. And depending on things like our types of wounds, how many we have, our personality, and lots of other factors, our idol choices will vary. What completely entangles me might be something you wouldn't cross the street for and vice versa.

My personal experience has taught me that it's not enough to merely walk away from our functional gods. To some degree, I believe it's important to understand what got us there in the first place, so we can halt repeating visits. And the one thing that seems consistent across the board is that our pain will make us cross the street for whatever idol promises relief.

Author Anne Lamott writes, "Almost everyone [is] struggling to wake up, to be loved, and not feel so afraid all the time. That's what the cars, degrees, booze, and drugs [are] about."[9]

My consistent travel schedule keeps me acquainted with the profound pain in people's lives—their desire to escape loneliness, wake up, and be loved. I greet it in different cultures, ages, colors. Miriam, married for fifty-six years, just lost her husband; Kelsey suffers from cerebral palsy; Rose was abused as a child and is now bipolar; Phu lives in a hut after losing both parents to AIDS; Trey is fighting terminal lung cancer; and Angel, the four-pound baby I held last week, was found on the street in the arms of her wandering, cocaine-addicted mother—umbilical cord still attached. Who's not looking for a little relief?

A friend of mine from high school is now a nurse in China. After spending last summer in the States, she sent me an e-mail describing the pain she saw in America as "deep, private, unanticipated, suffocating." And that deep, private, unanticipated, suffocating pain will make anyone especially susceptible to idol seduction. The unmanageable hurt creates a hunger for relief, desperation for our thirst to be slaked. Anything to pluck us from the misery—even if it's for an hour, a night, or a few good years.

o   o   o

I met up for coffee with a friend in Boston. Ashley is a stunning brunette who wakes up beautiful, the kind who emerges from her covers with hair pleasantly disheveled, every strand perfectly out of place. I always feel abnormally puffy and pasty around people like this, much more aware of whatever eyebrow I haven't plucked. Usually in these situations I order a colossal mug of tea that I can hold with dignity in front of my face—I feel more attractive when less of me is showing.

Though remarkably stunning on the outside, Ashley's beauty does not mirror inward ease. She's had a hard and uphill road, marred with abuse and abandonment. It has left her vulnerable to cravings for unhealthy men, one right after the other. As we sat across the table from each other, Ash filled me in on her latest man, while I felt increasingly fat. She had gone four years without an unhealthy male relationship since completing a nine-month program for abused women. That is, four years until the ten days before we met up in Boston.

"Kelly, I have met the sweetest guy in the world. He doesn't love God like I do, but he's been coming to church with me. And when I met him he was doing drugs, but since we've been together he hasn't used once. I think it's so respectable he would do that for me." I intently nodded behind my exceptionally large tea, unsure of any words, desperately wishing we had gotten together just a few days earlier. Not that I could have talked her out of anything, but one vainly hopes.

As we continued in conversation she told me that she had slept with this guy the night before, and that it had been the first time she'd been with anyone since her recovery program. My body fell a little limp, a visceral response that was anything but condemning, just sad. She told me that she knew it was wrong but freely admitted that she didn't really care anymore. "I just want somebody so bad I can hardly breathe at night. I don't want to withhold from myself any longer."

I think Ashley was ready for me to drop a Bible on the table, tell her that sex outside marriage is destructive and sinful, and say to stop on a dime. I suppose I could have gone that route except that it was stuff she already knew. Truth that hadn't made it into her heart because her pain and desire to be loved and held was so overwhelming she would justify any man in sight. Truth that she only understood in a sterile, academic sort of way. She never grasped God's heart behind his creeds, his love behind his borders. After all, her cavernous longings had been satiated; for a night, she was not alone. But this momentary solution made a crude mockery of sincere love, one that left her a bit more desperate the next morning.

Ashley's words rushed over me like a fountain of desperation. My eyes brimmed with tears. Not because she had committed the big no-no of Christianity, but because she had missed Christ and had fallen before something totally incapable of healing her. Because she had given it all up—not just her body, but her story and her life—for someone she had known for ten whole days. As I stared at the table, I saw the most opportune crumb I've seen in a long time. "Ash, my heart is heavy because you gave you for this." I pointed at the crumb, perhaps feeling a thread of what is behind God's passionate jealousy for us to heed his voice. I didn't behold Ashley as someone who'd simply broken the rules, but saw a welding of flesh and soul that would be unbearable to pull apart, a remarkable woman—beautiful, other worldly in her compassion, warm and profoundly loved by God—who cast herself away for mere crumbs. That was the tragedy.

○   ○   ○

Ashley's abuse and rejection had set her up for this kind of god. Someone else's pain might have driven them to workaholism, drugs, overeating, *Friends* reruns. For me, my brokenness propelled me to achieve and accomplish for insatiable amounts of approval. Who or what is the god before whose feet you have fallen? What can't you possibly live without? Where has your overwhelming hurt led you? Because our pain will always lead us somewhere, whether to false gods or to Christ.

Perhaps this is why Jesus said in Matthew 11:28, "Come to me, all you who are weary and burdened, and I will give you rest." He knows that the weary and burdened are going to go somewhere for relief, whether it's down the street to the bar, to an old boyfriend's house, the seductive magazine under the bed, the tawdry Web site, the kitchen with two-dozen doughnuts and the blinds drawn. Or to the broad arms of Christ, where he has specifically called us—the weary and the burdened—to come.

Jesus calls the place of his presence here a place of rest, but it's a little different than the rest of swaying on a hammock beachside. This rest requires that we take his yoke, which is easy and light. The word *yoke* is not something we toss around too often today, as it's an apparatus placed on cattle to join them to one another so they can pull something like a plow. Not really water-cooler talk. But the principle is so beautiful and vital to understanding what it means for God to be God in our life, as opposed to gods functioning as God. Metaphorically, the word is a picture of bondage or slavery, which doesn't sound particularly restful to me, sort of as exciting as sticking my head in a gallows. But if I can borrow from Romans 6:16 for a minute, the bottom line is that we are all slaves to something, whether to sin or to righteousness: "Don't you know that when you offer yourselves to someone to obey him as slaves, you are slaves to the one whom you obey—whether you are slaves to sin, which leads to death, or to obedience, which leads to righteousness?" Paul explains that whatever we obey—whatever we offer ourselves to—becomes our master.

When Ashley offered herself to her boyfriend, in a sense she became his slave. Not because she was living in a dated, chauvinistic society (it's Boston for heaven's sake), but because she attached herself to him by complex measures. Physically and emotionally she "yoked" herself. And this is not just about sex. Sex was just one more compounding piece that made her just a little more of a slave. And if you could have heard the panicked desperation in her voice, the I-can't-live-without-him tone, you would have gotten the impression that if for some reason he decided to leave her, say, for more drugs perhaps, he would be walking off with the ring of keys to her life. It is the same with me—when I strive endlessly for the approval of others, the people I am striving for become my masters.

So in essence, Christ counters this type of living with, "Come be a slave to me. My yoke is easy and my burden is light." According to Paul in Romans, we all have a yoke and we all have a burden—there is no getting around this, as much as we might like to think we can skip through life weightless and independent. Every day, every minute, we will serve something. The trickier part is who or what will that be? Jesus continues in Matthew 11:29: "Take my yoke upon you and learn from me, for I am gentle and humble in heart, and you will find rest for your souls." The idols of our hearts—the people I depend on for approval, Ashley's dismal boyfriend, five more social drinks—are not gentle, and they are far from humble. They are cruel with our hearts, promising what can't suffice yet grooming us as repeat customers. Their yoke is weighty and binding. Christ's is easy and light.

o     o     o

On the front end, it can seem like the contrary: It's the principles of obedience that can sometimes feel heavy and life-sucking, while the sparkle and promise of our favorite false god can look irresistible. The book of Proverbs tells us twice that there is a way that seems especially right to us, but in the end it leads to death. It's the glimmering raw steak on a clothesline that lures the unsuspecting cartoon character right off the cliff. In the end, the yoke that leads to destruction is not easy, nor its burden light.

When the Israelites left Egypt, they stepped out of slavery into an arid desert. Their desire for relief and a sense of settlement kicked in right on cue—immediately. They wanted off the hot sand and they wanted some real food, not the manna desert diet. They were primo candidates for some idol seduction, as places of pain, hunger, and a desire for relief will make any of us more vulnerable to false gods. Psalm 106:13–14 describes their situation this way: "But they soon forgot what he had done and did not wait for his counsel. *In the desert they gave in to their craving;* in the wasteland they put God to the test."

This is really huge to me. It doesn't say that they gave in to their craving while in the lap of luxury, or in the king's court, or in the Promised Land. It wasn't in the new house, or in the Mexican restaurant, or at the hotel suite overlooking South Beach. They gave in to their craving in the desert. In the heat. In the hunger. In the pain. Later in this psalm is where we find verse 36, which we looked at earlier: "They worshiped their idols, which became a snare to them." This snare is the heavy and burdensome yoke of false gods. It's the snare that hooked my friend Ashley. It's the snare that's gotten me a time or two or thousand. It's the nail Scott has in his pocket.

If you find yourself treading upon the hot sand, craving relief and satisfaction, you may become especially vulnerable to the bidding of false gods. It's in these times of desperation that most of us are more likely to circle back to the deceiving comforts of our past, willing to try anything that might smooth the edge off. But it is also in these times that we need to especially guard our hearts, to recognize our vulnerability and fortify our belief in God, remind ourselves of his love and faithfulness to us, remembering his yoke—the one that is attached to Christ. As Psalm 106:13 reads, life would have been wondrously different for the Israelites had they waited for God's counsel.

This is the yoke of Christ: being bound to his guidance and instruction, as two people walking hand in hand, though in this case his steady yoke is much more secure than our finicky hands. When we take this binding, yet mysteriously freeing, yoke upon ourselves, we naturally follow his commands and find that indeed they are not burdensome (1 John 5:3), but life-giving, truth-telling, and freedom-granting. "Be still before the Lord and wait patiently for him" (Ps. 37:7).

# 7

# LOVED LESS

Though pain in general is a significant force that drives us to our idols, I've noticed a few specific forms in particular that seem to put us on the fast track to them. I have found, both personally and from others, that the powerful ache of being unloved or perpetually unchosen is a paramount reason to turn to cruel impostors instead of to Christ. And the pandemic of unloved children and adults seems on the rise as babies are born into dysfunctional families, and spouses are the victims of affairs and divorces, or even of marriages that stay together but in an eternally icy state. Not to mention abuse, or the common but devastating feeling of simply being left out of friendships or going years without ever being asked out.

Several months ago I was headed back to my hotel room in Ft. Lauderdale after a long rehearsal. I was feeling the weightiness of extended travel and separation from friends. I could make it more complicated, but in essence I was sad. I don't always have this urge, but when I got to my room I curled up in the token chair that's supposed to make you feel like you're home—except that no one has chairs like these in their living rooms—and I began to peruse the life of Jacob in Genesis. Normally some chocolate cake or a movie will do the trick, but this was a sadness beyond the reach of even frosting and Tom Hanks. I needed to hear God speak. And for some reason, I took comfort in the fact that the winding, straying, plain defiant path of Jacob was within the infinite reach of God's love. His story seemed like the perfect remedy for my lonely state, the medicine of God's sovereignty across life's jagged terrain.

What I didn't know was that God had entirely different characters from Jacob to better acquaint me with, sort of like going to a friend's party where you end up meeting a whole new crowd. Rachel and Leah were the two sisters I found on the patio eating chips and drinking, say, iced tea. Besides Leah having a thousand kids, we all had a lot in common. If you have a minute to read Genesis 29:31—30:24, I think you would enjoy meeting them firsthand. They're worth the introduction, plus their stories are messier than television—with God remaining intimately involved in their lives—which affords hope to us all. I, at least, am encouraged by this notion.

Their story also appealed to me out of its innate twistedness. Lots of entangling emotions and wants wrapped themselves like strands of yarn around their relationships, no one piece especially strong but collectively more daunting than a steel cord. Only God could deliver from such misery, and in that I took hope.

Both Rachel and Leah had difficult plights; for starters, they were sisters married to the same man, Jacob, and I've never known this to be a particularly healthy setup, though at least it was more common back then. Jacob, however, was about the only thing they shared, as their roads forked pretty sharply after their connection with him. Rachel was the chosen one, the victor of Jacob's affection, the beautifully endowed of the two. You can almost hear the gossip of new acquaintances leaving the scene: "Rachel is so stunning. Hard to believe Leah's her sister!" Every word whispered in that "bless her heart" kind of tone.

Although Rachel held the beauty and husband cards, the ace of children was maddeningly absent from her hand. By the anger and resentment recorded in Genesis, you might have thought she'd be willing to toss her looks and husband out for one shot at a baby, her heightened frustration doubling every ten seconds, which was how often Leah churned out another child. But this was little consolation for the older, not so attractive sister who might have sold her children for Jacob to—just once—gaze at her with longing and dazzled eyes. Rachel and Leah both had what the other wanted, neither content with her own lot.

Although I find bits of myself in each of them, I am most intimately acquainted with Leah's struggle to be chosen and loved. I relate to the heights to which she went to acquire something you can never acquire on your own—another's love. There are no hoops you can leap through, no oceans to traverse that can ever make a person love you. And Leah certainly proved for the rest of us that no amount of childbearing will do it either—thank God we can scratch this one off the list.

And even though we're given to the attempt to secure love by our own efforts, doesn't all this striving miss the whole point of love anyhow? If we could make someone love us, it wouldn't be love after all.

My friend Kathy and I have mulled this one over on many a walk. Beautiful, hilarious, loyal, and super-high unleaded octane is Kathy—after all these years I have finally discovered where all my missing energy went, coiled up in her DNA, I think. She told me about a guy she was in love with who just couldn't quite reciprocate. She was at her perfect weight, excelling in her career and singing like a songbird. Perhaps he wanted a belly dancer instead of a singer, someone low-key instead of fun times. The Kathy Show, though at standing-room capacity, for some reason never sold a ticket to Kevin. I think sometimes she laments how hard she tried.

The progression of Leah's desperation and striving for Jacob's love is told through the names of her children. Her first son she named Reuben, which in Hebrew sounds like "he has seen my misery," and she said, "Surely my husband will love me now" (Gen. 29:32). For those of us who have experienced the futility of trying to win someone's love by what we could bring to the table, this feels especially tragic. Two sons later she gave birth to Levi, whose name in Hebrew means "attached," and she said, "Now at last my husband will become attached to me" (29:34).

o   o   o

Many years ago I had a counselor/friend who "chose" me for a season. Her affection for me was decorated with phone calls, gifts, lingering talks. She was a woman of power, while I was a fledgling writer, singer, speaker, fence painter, lawn mower, coach, babysitter. Her attention was like what I imagine a sniff of cocaine to be, a bit electric on the front end, but not so great for the rest of your life. Eventually another person traversed her path who was a little more exciting than me, a lot more established, sans the neediness. My friend wasted no time in backing away from me like she was fleeing the scene of a fire, swiftly latching onto the next fresh person.

I felt like my legs had been swiped out from under me, as if I had really gotten somewhere until I realized that my forward movement had been her legs carrying me on her terms. Sadly, the fact that I had lost her "love" didn't register as a showstopper for me; the curtains were drawn, the audience had filed out while I still sat in the dark hoping for another scene. Because of a few things she actually still needed me for, I, like Leah, was willing to downgrade my expectation for love and settle for mere attachment. I'm wincing as I write about such a painful ride.

So I identify with Leah when she bore Zebulun, son number six (or number eight if you include the two from her slave girl that counted as Leah's), and said, "This time my husband will treat me with honor" (30:20). It was the bottom of a downward slope that began with a desire to be loved, dropped to a longing to be merely attached to, and finally ended with the hope for a little respect from the man whom she loved so desperately and who had fathered her many children. It's as if she'd given up on the steak and was contending for the fried chicken on the kids' menu. When Jacob is your god, you have no other choice.

I wish the story perked up a little here, but this is where if Leah were in a movie, all the women in the theater would be covering their eyes and sighing, "Don't do it, you're worth more!" Yes, Leah traded Rachel mandrake plants for sex with Jacob. (If my movie idea pans out, the producers will have to modernize this a bit, as I think this might have been the last time a mandrake was sold for something like this.) Mandrakes were believed to increase fertility, which goodness knows Leah didn't need any more of but which was a real commodity for Rachel. "So when Jacob came in from the fields that evening, Leah went out to meet him. 'You must sleep with me,' she said. 'I have hired you with my son's mandrakes.' So he slept with her that night" (30:16).

Even the anxiousness of running out to meet him in the field strikes me as a new low of desperation for Leah. The fact that it wasn't his choice, that she had to ask permission from her younger sister, and that she had to sell something for a faint expression of Jacob's affection is a disturbing picture. Not to mention she got pregnant yet again out of the deal, which I'm sure just steamed Rachel as she sat barren despite those mandrakes decorating the kitchen. And yet no matter how many children Leah had, she couldn't remedy the one cry of her heart—her desire to be exclusively loved by Jacob.

Genesis 29:30 lays it out in shocking clarity: "Jacob lay with Rachel also, and he loved Rachel more than Leah." Which can also be translated, "He loved Leah less than Rachel."

If any of Leah's story is resonating with you, I'm assuming at some point in your life you have been loved less. You have experienced the harrowing ache of bringing all you had, only to come in second or third or twenty-ninth to Rachel. You've hung your heart on the one person you were sure could give you life but never did. You threw down your finest, only for someone to pass it over like the fruitcake on a Christmas spread.

o   o   o

I remember being in college and falling for a guy who had taken an interest in me. He was popular, athletic, funny, and kind. He was the first attractive man, at least in my mind, who had ever really chosen me. We never officially "dated"—whatever that means in college, or for heaven's sake whatever that means now—but we did almost everything together and I think that's supposed to count for something. Over a year's time my heart became attached to his, his features having grown ever more charming. That's right around the time he had the "I don't think I can commit to you/you're a great friend/this is not about you, blah, blah, blah" chat with me. Months later he started dating the woman he ended up marrying, which always makes you think that maybe it was just a little about you.

If you're sadder than you were before you entered into my sadness and Leah's sadness at the top of the chapter, may I interest you in some chocolate cake or a movie? Actually a more significant remedy is on its way. One that comes from the God of gods, who cannot by virtue of his very essence, and will not by virtue of his character, love you less.

But to grasp this love experientially, you have to throw in the towel on Jacob, demoting him from Godlike status. You have to give up on the belief that Jacob or Tom or Kevin or a friend can save the day, embracing at a gut level that wholeness can only be accomplished, interestingly enough, by the God of Jacob.

That night in my Florida hotel room I met Leah and really got to know her, at least as much as you can in a couple chapters. If I could transcend time and history, appearing on Leah's front stoop for a leisurely soul-chat would be high on my list. I mean, don't get me wrong, a visit with Ruth, Hannah, Esther, and Deborah would be pretty amazing, but there's something about a woman who withstood a lifetime of less love that I would be the richer to hear from. And if I can get really picky in my imagination, I would prefer to sit down with her many years beyond where the account of her life ends. I'm curious to know where she arrived after bearing all those children. I wonder if she ever settled into the idea that she might not ever be chosen—at least not by Jacob—and that perhaps this was the most liberating conclusion she could ever come to. Liberating, because she would finally be free of needing to secure his love for survival and would now be open to the only love that could feed life in her. I wonder if she ever realized that Jacob's love was actually not the key to her wholeness. Or if she eventually came back around to that sweet space she had found in child number four, Judah, the child that made her proclaim, "This time I will praise the LORD." The account continues: "Then she stopped having children."

Perhaps this can also be translated, "Then she stopped trying to gain Jacob's favor (for a while)." Or maybe it wasn't Leah's decision to stop having children but was the Lord who temporarily closed her womb, desiring that her attention be turned to him. When Judah was born, she recognized for a season that her children were precious gifts from God, love notes from her Creator, not means by which to secure her husband's affection but beautiful ends in themselves.

It's impossible to know exactly where Leah ended up on her journey for love, but there are significant details stemming from her life worth mentioning. We have the benefit of being able to see generations down the road, peering into a moment that Leah could have never put together in an eternity of dreams: the birth of Jesus Christ, miraculously born of Mary, who was married to Joseph, who was born of Jacob, born of Matthan, born of Eleazar, born of Eliud, born of Akim, born of Zadok, born of Azor, born of Eliakim, born of Abiud, born of Zerubbabel, born of Shealtiel, born of Jeconiah, born of Josiah, born of Amon, born of Manasseh, born of Hezekiah, born of Ahaz, born of Jotham, born of Uzziah, born of Jehoram, born of Jehoshaphat, born of Asa, born of Abijah, born of Rehoboam, born of Solomon, born of David, born of Jesse, born of Obed, born of Boaz, born of Salmon, born of Nahshon, born of Amminadab, born of Ram, born of Hezron, born of Perez, born of Judah—born of Jacob and Leah.

The Christ child, the Savior to the world, both past and present, was born through Leah's child. And when Jacob was on his deathbed he asked Joseph, the son of his wife Rachel, to carry his body from Egypt back to Canaan and bury him next to—not Rachel, but Leah. I wonder if all those years before, Leah ever imagined that Rachel's firstborn, Joseph, would be the one to carry her husband back to her side for burial, if she ever thought that she and Jacob, when all was said and done, would lie together in the company of Abraham and Sarah, Isaac and Rebekah.

I wonder if Leah ever grasped within her lifetime that though Jacob had chosen Rachel, God had chosen her.

○   ○   ○

Perhaps you find yourself not only striving for a person's love, but for God's as well. Perhaps, like Leah, your gaze is tangled up on a human savior because you've missed the supernatural One who longs for you to comprehend his love. This is not always easy, because we can viscerally see, touch, and hold people, while God can at times feel distant. This is where the physical person of Jesus Christ enters big for us— God who was made man.

I remember going through a Bible study during my teen years that asked two significant questions relating to this topic. The first was "Do you love God?" I meticulously filled in the blank with an easy yes. However, the second question threw me for an unexpected loop: "Do you know that God loves you?" The simple reverse of the question became far more complex for me—I distinctly remember not being able to answer, knowing in my head that the correct response was yes, but struggling in my heart to emphatically write that I believed this.

Years have since transpired, making that a much simpler question for me to answer honestly. I do know that God loves me, much of the time I feel that he loves me, and on some days I can almost palpably sense his love. A few of the things that have helped grow the security of this knowledge for me have been time in Scripture, time with others who love him deeply, time in prayer, and simply experiencing life with him.

Reading and contemplating Scripture has been invaluable, as I've kept an eye out for the ways he has shown his people love, journaling about their stories and rehearsing them in my mind when I'm tempted to think otherwise. Also, the time I've spent with godly men and women who have shared remarkable accounts of his faithfulness and mercy to them—even in the most traumatic and darkest of times—has been of priceless benefit. And, of course, the many prayers I have prayed that somewhere included, "Lord, show me your love," have indeed been answered. And just a side note here: If you have trouble praying alone, do it with others, because the confidence and passion that comes with praying in a group, or even with one other person, has been of great help to me.

Lastly, there is no substitute for simply believing that God is love. As 1 John 3:1 so beautifully puts it, "How great is the love the Father has lavished on us, that we should be called the children of God! *And that is what we are!*" If such belief is difficult for you, as it has been for me at times, you are in good company. As one man said to Jesus, "I do believe; help me overcome my unbelief!" (Mark 9:24), so too can we cry out the same beautifully human words.

I so wonder if Leah was ever this honest with the Lord about her difficult plight. Though hers is a sad story of jealousy and unrequited love, a subtle yet prominent character reigned above the narrative.

God, in his unfailing love, blessed Leah with children, chose her to be the woman from whose seed Jesus Christ would come, and allowed Rachel's son Joseph to lay Jacob next to her in burial. It seems that despite such acts, she missed the favor and love of God as she sought for such treasure through her empty pursuit of Jacob, the idol of her heart.

It makes me wonder what I am missing in my own obsessive chases of what cannot satisfy. This is not to cheapen the inordinate value of having a spouse, friend, child, or family member love you. Human love is God-given and to be celebrated. It's needful for life. Certainly God would not command us to love one another, or be so forceful on the importance of loving your wife or husband or children and being faithful to them at all costs, if human love was optional. But if seeking the love of a person becomes the ultimate thing, if it takes the place of seeking the love of God, if it becomes the first and most prominent pursuit of our lives, everything gets out of order and begins to fall in on itself. God still must sit at the top of the chain. It reminds me of the familiar verse, "Seek first [God's] kingdom and his righteousness, and all these things will be given to you as well" (Matt. 6:33).

Without the slightest hint of condemnation for Leah—remember, we are friends now—I wonder what life would have looked like for her if she had sought God as her all in all ahead of Jacob. I have experienced both pursuits in my life and have found that when I seek him first, he lavishly provides the delight and beauty of human love, but when I get this backward, I am empty on both accounts. It's sort of like

C. S. Lewis's brilliant words: "Aim at heaven and you will get earth thrown in. Aim at earth and you get neither."[10]

For those who have been loved less, who have been abandoned by parents as children (or adults), who have been abused, left out of friendship circles, remain unchosen, my prayer is that you will not give up but seek the God whose very essence is love. The Bible tells us that he is a father to the fatherless, he places the orphans in families, and he puts an unprecedented premium on loving one another. It is important to God that people love you, but it is more important that you come to experientially understand that he loves you. When you grasp even a modicum of the height, depth, and width of such love, your idols will grow strangely faint, pitifully powerless compared to God, whose very nature is love.

# 8

# NOT ENOUGH

Unattained love is a prominent catalyst behind our search for idols, as it was in Leah's life of desperation for Jacob, a false god who could never satisfy her. It is no stretch to see how such emptiness could propel anyone to pursue myriad solutions, so often apart from God. After acquainting myself with Leah, I found her story sad but one that at least made sense. It was Rachel's that posed more difficulty for me, as I'm always fascinated by the person who seemingly has it all yet is on a perpetual search for just one more thing—certain it will fill the void they were sure the last thing was going to fill. And yet as soon as I write that, I realize that simply by living in America, in many ways I indeed have it all, yet continually ache for more. Perhaps I am not as far from her as I may deem.

Rachel, in many ways the flipside of Leah, was a has-it-all kind of girl yet was arguably as miserable as her rejected sister—incidentally with an extra side of anger. At first this confused me, considering she had everything Leah wanted and was convinced would make her happy: Jacob's exclusive love, not to mention stunning beauty. Of course, there is the part about her not being able to have any children for a long time. It's certainly reasonable to assume her misery stemmed from such a significant vacancy, especially in light of Leah's factory-esque production of them, like being a diabetic living next door to a candy store.

Rachel's lack of children must have pierced her as deeply as Leah's lack of love. If only Rachel could have had children and Leah could have had Jacob, it's almost plausible to think that both could have achieved happiness—if nothing else, it would have made for a bang-up reality series. If Leah's idol was Jacob, Rachel's was having children. Neither are bad things in themselves; in fact, both husbands and children are profoundly good things, indeed desirable things. But when those things, or anything, take the place of God in our lives, when they become the ultimate things, when they become all consuming, they become false; they become little-*g* gods.

In case you're not sure what being all consumed by something looks like, as much as I appreciate Rachel, she gives us a pretty decent picture at the top of Genesis 30: "When Rachel saw that she was not bearing Jacob any children, she became jealous of her sister. So she said to Jacob, 'Give me children, or I'll die!'" How this suddenly became Jacob's sole responsibility is a bit of a mystery to me, especially considering the number of kids he had already fathered—the problem didn't seem to lie with him. But desperation has been known to lead to irrationality, and sometimes you just need something, or think you need it, so painfully bad that you start making ridiculous and impossible demands of people.

o o o

I saw this at the Denver airport a few months ago: I was on my way home, or thought I was on my way, until an airline that will remain nameless failed to get me home for the who-knows-how-many-eth time, bumping me off the flight. What especially intrigues me about air travel is that your compensation for such debacles is always the same: a free ticket to relive the nightmare on the same crummy airline. It's like, give me a ticket on another airline, or a helicopter, or a boat, or something—anything but rewarding me with yourselves again.

I am truly blessed to have the Holy Spirit in these situations, though I'm not sure I'm the easiest for him in these moments. The woman in front of me was handling her frustration in a slightly different manner, simply with the most colossal-sized beer I have ever seen someone drink with a straw. I seriously have no idea where she found such a thing in a place where items like lipstick and tweezers are banned. She nursed the thing through the serpentine line of angry travelers that was long enough, while the cup was deep enough, to deposit her at the customer-service desk in a slightly altered state. She wasn't on my flight, so I was interested to hear if her misfortune was similar to mine.

We both stepped up to different agents simultaneously. I took that deep breath that you take—the one that separates a mere heightened mood from complete insanity—and calmly (though secretly crazy-mad) asked to be rebooked. The woman next to me didn't take that breath.

"I demand you put me on the next flight out of here."

"Ma'am, we can't help that you were in the bathroom when your flight boarded and took off," the agent actually said with a straight face.

"That's not acceptable," she replied.

"Well, ma'am, we have no other flights headed to Omaha this evening. I can get you out first thing in the morning."

"Put me on another airline then!" She slapped her hand on the table.

"I'm so sorry, but we can't do that. Even if we could, there are no more flights leaving tonight."

"That's not good enough!"

"That's not good enough" became her go-to line every time the poor agent opened his mouth. As if he was supposed to wiggle his nose for a chartered plane. I have no idea what kind of power she thought his uniform afforded him. Short of putting her in his car and driving her, he was out of options, yet she continued to demand that he do something he had no power to do. The scene built to purely entertaining proportions until she finally yelled some very unprintable and unkind words to the agent and stormed off.

After gathering myself from the sheer magnitude of the scene, I became mindful of how ridiculously and unreasonably demanding people will get—I will get—when we become desperate for something we are certain we need. Rachel's wild anger flared in Jacob's face simply because he couldn't provide her with the impossible. When something we're consumed with is at stake, something we simply must have, we often irrationally demand in ways that not only expose our obscene desperation but put impossible expectations on those we're looking to.

While growing up, I demanded from my parents, and more recently from my friends, things they simply are not capable of providing me with. The last few years have been a boot camp in learning to dialogue and seek the Lord when—I can't believe it—people aren't meeting my needs.

o   o   o

If my choices aren't this wise, I've also been known to take matters into my own hands, as if airport-lady had grabbed her bags and started walking east. This was the case with Rachel, who was so bent on getting children one way or another that she decided that having them through her slave girl might suffice. Although I believe her desire for children was deep and sincere, it's noteworthy that the verse says, "When Rachel saw that she was not bearing Jacob any children, she became jealous of her sister." We see this envious strain run throughout the next few verses as we read Rachel's reaction to the two children her slave girl, Bilhah, gave her: "I have had a great struggle with my sister, and I have won" (30:8).

This statement exposes the stream of pain running through Rachel's life. Though she spoke it with force, you can almost feel her shaky cry for significance, her plea for identity. Part of Rachel's inordinate desire to get pregnant was born out of something that is difficult for us to understand in modern Western civilization. Though most people today still highly value the ability to bear children, it's hard to compare it to the significance it held in ancient times. For Rachel, her beauty was worthless without children of her own, because a barren woman was a failure as a woman as far as her society was concerned. And it wasn't simply that a barren woman missed the joy of family and children—she was humiliated, less-than, and deemed by her peers as worthless. This depth of pain is hard for us to grasp, and it somewhat explains her impassioned outbursts at Jacob and her schemes to achieve quasi motherhood through her slave girl, Bilhah. (It was an acceptable custom in those days to give a slave girl to one's husband and to take ownership of the offspring. However, it should be noted that "acceptable" didn't necessarily mean satisfying or right.)

Jacob was not enough for Rachel. Not even his undivided, focused love. Her attractive physique was not sufficient; she held no consolation in being more beautiful than Leah, nor did she have any in being more loved. She was determined to have the only thing Leah had, the only thing she didn't have: children. And when she finally got a couple under her roof, ones that weren't biologically hers, she proclaimed that she had struggled with Leah and had won!

It's interesting to note that though Rachel had proclaimed herself the winner, it was Leah's four children to Rachel's slave girl's two. (Interesting arithmetic for sure.) Her need to keep score exposes her insecurity, and her inability to keep it accurately shows an even deeper desperation. I in no way mean to denigrate Rachel, and in fact my heart is tugged for her, but I just don't think we can gloss over her jealousy, emptiness, insecurity, anger, and competitiveness, as it's a profound window into our own lives. She almost had it all, yet still she was miserable.

We can conclude this, because God eventually opened Rachel's womb, making her the mother of Joseph and Benjamin, yet the story doesn't leave us convinced that this was enough. It's logical to think that these would be the moments of completion for her. It's easy to assume she found contentment after officially attaining it all: love, beauty, and children. She was living the American dream in Paddan Aram. What more could one want? Perhaps here we would expect to get the tidy moral to such a seemingly sad and unresolved story: Those who are beautiful and desired by men are happy, and those who are homely and unloved are miserable. It's a message that seems to fit snugly with our culture, though not a terribly helpful takeaway if you happen to be more like Leah and a little less like beautiful, prosperous, loved Rachel.

Though it's hard to measure Rachel's level of contentment at this point, we catch a glimpse of something that tells us her heart was still grasping for fulfillment. A few verses later, in Genesis 31:19 (when Jacob, his wives, and children were all fleeing Rachel's father, Laban), we find Rachel raiding her father's house and stealing his household gods. The technical name is teraphins, which are small images found in the homes of that day. I'm not sure out of all the things Rachel could have taken why she chose her father's gods, but I think it says something significant about her.

After sitting with Rachel's story for a time, the fact that she was swiping miniature gods on the way out of town, ones that weren't even hers, tells much about the lack of contentment in her heart. As she left her father, she walked away a beautiful woman. She left with a husband who not only loved her but chose her. She mounted the camel that was carrying a child who had come from her own womb, and yet still something was missing. Maybe she thought a quick rummage through the house for a few idols might do the trick. If nothing else, it exposed two things about a woman who seemingly had it all: that she hadn't fully turned to the God of Israel, and that she was still looking for sufficiency elsewhere.

Leah's story is one of obvious heartbreak and misery, while Rachel's is a bit more veiled, perhaps not eliciting as much sympathy. It's harder to bleed for the Hollywood stars, harder to feel sorry for the rich and beautiful, for mothers of sons like Joseph.

Though most of us can probably relate more easily to Leah's misery of having less, there have undoubtedly been times when we've finally gotten that one thing we wanted yet felt strangely void. The sensation may have even led us to the next idol, whatever we could get our hands on, like Rachel stuffing gods into her backpack on the way back to Canaan. (Laban ended up chasing Jacob for those idols later in the narrative, and as my pastor, Jim Thomas, so eloquently put it last Sunday, "If your god can be stolen, he's probably not that great of a god.")

o    o    o

After my mini breakdown in my Ft. Lauderdale hotel room, and my subsequent evening with Rachel and Leah, my brain gave up a lot of space for mulling. I wondered what the point of this story was. Leah had little and was miserable; Rachel had everything and was miserable. It appeared a dead-end story with no meaning.

I don't remember exactly when it happened, but as I continually questioned the point, I remember hearing the subtle voice of the Holy Spirit say, "That is the point."

"What's the point, Lord? They both led remarkably sad lives, at least as much as is revealed."

I acknowledged it again: "That is the point."

It wasn't long after that the whole thing finally dawned on me. But before I get there, I don't want to imply that there's only one moral, or that all stories in the Bible have to have some neat and tidy principle at the end, some three-point wrap-up. I am confident that there are theological gems tucked throughout the many layers of this account that I will never get to. This is neither the first nor the final word on Rachel and Leah, yet it is revelation to my heart from what I understand to be God-inspired: It matters little if you have it all or if you have less—without Christ, wholeness is but a fantasy.

The two sisters are beautifully painted juxtapositions—different looks, loves, and abilities mirroring desperate dispositions. I realized that what a person has is of no consequence, whether much or little, when it comes to the deep satisfaction of the soul. Apart from Christ, the rich and beautiful, and the poor and unlovely, will all end up in precisely the same misery.

Through my acquaintance with Rachel and Leah, I began to revel in the understanding that Christ is everything. Satisfaction, wholeness, and peace are impossible without him. Leah in her destitution and Rachel in her abundance could have both been fulfilled by him. Yet they struggled to obtain more and grasped at the idols of husbands and children and literal figurines, never understanding that the God who saw Leah and the God who remembered Rachel was the fulfillment of their hearts' longing.

If you are loved less, he is the Great Provider. If you are loved more but are still hungry, he is the only One who can suffice.

# 9

# LIES

Like a swirling current, our pain does a great job of driving us to our false gods, but the false gods themselves do an equally good job of wooing us. If pain is a push toward our idols, deceit is a pull from them. Of course, they can't do this by just standing there—they usually have to dress themselves up a little, flash a bit, sparkle some. They hide beneath stunning cloaks of deceit, promising us the world but giving us something more like bondage and devastation. Lies are another "why" behind our run to idols, and if we aren't aware of them, we will be fooled as easily as Eve standing amid a garden of food, reaching for the only tree that couldn't nourish her appetite.

I just returned from a trip to Ireland, a luscious deviation from bill paying and grocery shopping and e-mail returning. It is one of the few places I've been where I literally found myself inhaling the scenery, like if I breathed in the green grass and the fluffy sheep and the craggy ocean line it might be similar to drawing in essential oils like mint or eucalyptus. And if I could just learn to sing my words like the Irish, flipping up the tail ends of my sentences while cupping a fresh mug of tea, wisps of red hair falling across my face, perhaps life would be a little more of what it's supposed to be.

I was there to sing for a live worship recording that took place in a cozy theater moments from the north shore. The band was stellar, made up of world-class players, possibly none as gripping as Troy, player of the uilleann pipes. His mastery of such a haunting instrument was mesmerizing, the kind of thing that puts your life to a soundtrack if you're vulnerable enough to let it. Awestruck, I sank deeper into the rickety theater seats, the pipes' distinct timbre wrapping itself around me like an aroma, content to listen for as many moments as he might indulge me. As my producer friend likes to say, "Troy makes me happy I have ears." He also makes me happy I still have the ability to be dumbfounded, wonderstruck like a child whose cookies and milk had vanished on Christmas Eve.

And this wasn't simply because of his musicianship, but surprisingly because of the shocking magic tricks he'd pull out for us every evening in the bistro of the hotel. Up his uilleann-pipe-playing sleeve were endless mind-stunting card tricks, disappearing acts, utensils that moved across the table—*by themselves!* At one point he handed me a small stack of cards and asked me to count them. I was never a whiz at math, but a little counting I feel good about. With all the cards in my possession I flipped exactly ten onto the table. Then—without

Troy touching any of the cards—he asked me to sit on them. A few seconds later, after a couple of rousing stories and a couple of good shuffles of the rest of the deck, he told me to take the cards I had been sitting on and count them again. This time there were seven—with the three missing ones now mysteriously in his hand. Seriously. This was no pull the coin out from behind your ear or "pick a card, any card" type thing—I had been *sitting* on the cards for the love of all things!

I was astounded but skeptical. I tried to refrain from oohing and ahhing too much, hating to be as wide-eyed as I was feeling. The logical part of my brain desperately wanted to kick in but couldn't find so much as a crack of space to squeeze into. I knew that what I was seeing and experiencing was impossible, yet everything pointed to its reality. It was maddening really, and my annoyance spurred Troy on all the more. He kept after me with trick after trick, goading my skepticism with invitations like, "Kelly, last night I invented a new one just for you." Again he'd blow my mind.

After a few days of mini magic shows in the bistro, Troy, my friend April, and I found ourselves in the same vehicle on the way to rehearsal. The venue was only a few minutes away—plenty of time for Troy to tangle my mental faculties into a rat's nest yet again. With no visuals whatsoever he asked April to simply name a card. With saucer eyes and a giddy smile she called out the two of diamonds. I am telling the truth when I say that Troy reached into his pocket and pulled out a deck of all blue-backed cards except one red-backed card that happened to be, of course, the two of diamonds. I was so flipped out I wanted to start casting demons out of the guy. I implored him to explain how he had done it, as if my sanity and spiritual peace were resting on his explanation.

Like any good magician he never gave away his secrets, but he did admit to leading us the entire way. He said that both April and I were completely oblivious to the ways he had guided our minds along certain paths. He told me to listen to his words the next time he performed the trick for someone else, implying that its success lay not in the supernatural realm but in his ability to, in a sense, manipulate us unknowingly. Now I have no idea how this logic transfers to cards escaping from underneath me or forks skipping across the table, but I do know that every single trick was an illusion. This perhaps is what fascinates me even more than the tricks themselves, that I can be this misled with all of my wits about me, not passively engaged but actively looking for answers, inspecting every move, all to no avail.

The spiritual parallel doused me like a bucket of cold water, its truths trickling down into all this talk of false gods, reminding me of how deceptive they inherently are. How seamlessly our idols wield such attractive lies, dancing their illusions across our paths—never for the sake of simple entertainment, but instead for the precarious sake of captivity and destruction. How deeply duped I have been by the Father of Lies—the one who prowls around like a roaring lion looking for someone he can devour (1 Peter 5:8). Peter encourages us to be of a sober mind, on the alert, so as not to be taken by such deceptive devices. And unlike the secretive world of magic, Scripture is happy to expose the illusions of our most deceptive idols. It is the inspired text of God, written so that we might have the truth, and that such truth would set us free.

o   o   o

I'm not sure what most theologians would say, but I'm assuming that the lie originated in the garden of Eden. If it was around any earlier, I don't know about it. Most of us are familiar with the account of Adam and Eve in the garden, the deceiving Serpent, and the ensuing fall of man. I always knew that present in this passage were important pieces of history and theology that were fundamental to the Christian faith but didn't realize until recently how much there is that describes the human heart in a most practical way.

I've made it a practice, unintended, to visit biblical counselors in different seasons of my life. I have found it invaluable along the way, as the perspective of godly men and women who have been gifted to really "see" has deeply helped and encouraged me. There's been Ruth, Bill, Barbara, Al, and Larry—to name a few. Last year I was sitting in Larry's office, a pretty insightful guy who lives on a farm, wears Wrangler jeans and cowboy boots, and sometimes brings fresh eggs into the office. He swears by goat's milk that hasn't been pasteurized and eggs that have been laid in the last day or two. But these are just bonus suggestions.

I remember my first day in his office—they pretty much all start out the same. Usually the counselor is sitting in his chair with a deeply inquisitive look on his face and serenely begins with "So, why are you here?" At that point I usually start crying even if I'm not sad, because that's just what you do when you're in counseling. Seeing Larry was no exception even though we talked about cattle and organic dairy for the first twenty minutes. After I began explaining a few of the things I was going through, he asked me another question: "Can we go back to the beginning?" Since pretty much everyone's problems trace back to kindergarten, I was fine with that.

Interestingly enough, when I began at the beginning he kindly stopped me. "No, I mean the very beginning." I have a pretty keen memory but wasn't sure if I could remember that far back. Ages one and two are kind of fuzzy—I do remember getting "Ants in the Pants" for my birthday, and I think I was two when that happened, but maybe I was … It wasn't until he picked up his Bible, handed it to me, and had me turn to Genesis that I suddenly realized, Oh, that beginning! (The one just a little before "Ants in the Pants.") And can I just tell you that the ensuing conversation was one of the most therapeutic hours in counseling I've ever spent in my life?

I don't fully recall, but that first day I don't think we ever made it back to me and my problems. The study of God, Eve, Adam, the tree, and the Serpent gave me insight into my own life and struggles that I never knew could be culled from those pages of Scripture. So much of them seemed to tell the story not only of Adam and Eve, but of me, my heart, my passions, my longings, and the way I respond to both truth and deception. Over a year later I'm still finding new revelations surfacing from these pages. I want to share the ones that relate to the topic of this chapter, which are primarily on the lies that attach us to our idols.

One thing that overwhelmingly struck me was the subtle and crafty nature of Satan. It should come as no surprise, as the New Testament refers to him as the Father of Lies and a murderer from the beginning. But we touched on something just a little sneakier than anything I had noticed before, and it all began with the Serpent's question: "Did God really say …?" This was in reference to God's command not to eat from the Tree of the Knowledge of Good and Evil. I find it interesting that Satan didn't whisk in with a dogmatic statement—something like "God did not say" as opposed to "Did God say?" Nothing like a question to send your thoughts spinning into doubtful swirls.

When I think of the lies that I am prone to embrace, I realize that many of them begin as questions. It's not as often that I'm thrown by someone or something that comes right out and denounces my set of beliefs. Those are a lot easier to dismiss. But more often I am sent down a doubtful path when my beliefs are simply questioned. Because a statement doesn't require a response, but a question demands an answer. When a person or idea asks, "Did God really say?" suddenly we are in a state of thought, reason, and possible defense. A question engages us in ways that statements do not. I have to believe that Satan knew this.

But here's where things get trickier than I ever realized: Not only did the Serpent begin with a question, but his question was fundamentally flawed. "Did God really say, 'You must not eat from any tree in the garden'?" There's something eerily wrong with this question—notice the word *any*. God did not say that Adam and Eve couldn't eat from any tree in the garden. He said they could not eat from one. Just one. This is a world of difference. If Satan can lure us into disputing the wrong question, in a sense we have already lost.

I know this one too well. I have spent countless hours wasting my energy on things that didn't deserve it. I have spent exorbitant amounts of time fighting the wrong questions. Though I do not pretend the Christian life is neatly packaged or cut and dried, the Bible is full of countless truths that can keep me from having to enter countless unnecessary wrestling matches. Too many times I've limped away broken and bruised, only to hear God say, "I never asked you to fight this one."

When I ponder the times I have wrestled with lies, often I find myself set up in the same way Eve was—to fight the wrong question. The Serpent had set a faulty ground for her to wrestle on, knowing the question he wanted her to argue against was an incorrect one to begin with. If he could get her to believe that God had told her not to eat from any tree, suddenly she would have to defend against what wasn't true in the first place. Eve set herself apart here in that she didn't allow herself to get lassoed in; she silenced his question with the simple truth, in essence saying that God had told her she could eat from any tree in the garden, just not this one. At least here, Eve knew the truth and used it well. She forced the Serpent into round two, which incidentally didn't go as well, but that's another story....

o   o   o

Though Eve was solid in her response to the Serpent's initial question, she was deceived when she allowed him to take her focus off the truth and redirect it toward perhaps the most dangerous lie of all: You can be like God. It's worth taking note that Eve's gaze suddenly fell upon the fruit of the tree—Satan did not need to be the center of attention, merely to center her attention on anything else. This picture has inspired me to question the battles I weary myself in. How I long to cease entering the wrong fights and gazing at the wrong fruit. I am so desperately thankful for God's revelation.

It's been said that every lie has a little bit of truth in it, which is the magic ingredient that makes the whole thing so believable. I think that's why this next piece of the story is so intriguing to me. Verse 6 says, "The woman saw that the fruit of the tree was good for food and pleasing to the eye, and also desirable for gaining wisdom." By the time Eve got here, I think the deal was pretty much cinched. Because notice the three things Eve was certain the fruit was good for: food, beauty, and wisdom. She had stumbled upon something that appealed to her physical, emotional, and mental self. And is this not exactly what 1 John 2:16 (KJV) speaks of when it mentions the lust of the flesh (good for food), the lust of the eyes (pleasing to look upon), and the pride of life (desirable for gaining wisdom)? The fruit became the idol of Eve's heart. Just think of all it promised to do! And yet it was all a lie. Or was it? Perhaps the Serpent's claims were far truer than we ever considered.

A few months ago I was reading this passage, not imagining something new would arrest my senses. How I underestimate the Holy Spirit and the unsearchable riches of his wisdom. As I reassessed the three allures of this awful mighty piece of fruit—good for food, pleasing to the eye, and desirable for gaining wisdom—I realized something

I had never thought of before. As far as I could tell, all of these assessments were true! Explore with me.

First, the fruit was good for food. Even though Eve bit into a death sentence, it wasn't an immediate physical one. She didn't fall over from food poisoning. Second, it was pleasing to the eye. If it wasn't enticing and appetizing to look upon, she wouldn't have thought it so. Third— and probably the most surprising—the fruit was desirable for gaining wisdom. In Genesis 3:22 (after Adam and Eve had eaten of the tree), the Lord said, "The man has now become like one of us, knowing good and evil. He must not be allowed to reach out his hand and take also from the Tree of Life and eat, and live forever." Yes. Wisdom was gained. A wisdom we were never intended to gain by this means (by experiencing evil), but wisdom nonetheless. Eve's infamous conclusions were true after all. True, but not the truth.

I first heard this idea from Michael Wells, founder of Abiding Life Ministries International. I remember him saying that Satan will often tell us what is true, but will never tell us the truth. I could feel my brain synapses overfiring on this one. I thought of examples where I had been lured and hooked by things that were true, true, true, but—wait a minute—not the truth.

o     o     o

I know of a woman who is currently in the midst of an affair. She feels bad about it, but not bad enough to tell her husband and cut off the relationship. She has a few justifications that sound almost reasonable.

He treats me better than my husband does. Perhaps this is true. I'm more attracted to him than anyone I've ever met. I'm sure this is accurate. We have so much in common. Probably true. My husband can be a real jerk. True. It actually checks out pretty well. We have a lot of "trues" here. But we have one significant snag—to have an affair is never the truth.

If the lies of our idols attach us, the "trues" of our idols will absolutely devastate us. I suppose that is why God pleads with us to know the truth. Jesus says God's Word is truth (John 17:17). Though our struggle with lies and deception and false gods can at times be convoluted and entangling, the only effective tactic I have ever discovered is very simply the truth. Ultimately, that's what Eve finally strayed from.

Imagine, all this from a woman and a piece of fruit. Or was it the two of diamonds? It's all starting to run together....

So how can we tell if we're being lured by deceptive fruit, or card tricks, or a really bad boyfriend? Often we've lived with such things for so long they become hard to discern, so it's helpful to discover a few telling arrows that accurately point to our false gods. I call them idol signs, and they're excellent little navigators.

# (10)

# IDOL SIGNS

It was the loudest thing I had ever been on. Stifling loud. But then again, what did I expect a boat with an airplane propeller on the back was going to sound like? Apparently no one has invented silent airboats, at least not yet. But who wants to give up getting to wear those tough black headphones anyway? They're part of the costume really. Zipping through the Everglades like you're on ice, trouncing alligators, slicing through sawgrass like it's cotton candy—it just wouldn't be as validating without the gear, the headphones.

My Everglades adventures began with another friend named Scott, who is on staff at the church I frequently led worship at last summer in Florida. He owns his own airboat and asked if I'd be interested in a ride led by one of the most indigenous men to the area: Don, a grandfather of the Glades. My friends Margaret and April went with me, all of us having collectively traveled extensively—visiting villages in Swaziland, waking up to the stalwart Parthenon, sailing the Amazon, sipping coffee on the Mount of Olives—and yet the Everglades evoked an awe in us uniquely its own. No other location is in its class, from its ecosystem to the airboat, the only vehicle by which you can maneuver its daunting landscape.

Because of the deafening noise, I kept tapping Margaret on the shoulder from behind, pointing, mouthing unrecognizable words, widely smiling like I was five and it was my first trip to the zoo. April was born for such adventures and thus was a little more collected in her responses, gazing out over the landscape with a determined eye, sort of like at any moment she could whip out a fly-fishing rod or a shotgun.

Don was everything Scott had told us—a true expert of the territory, one who had lived in the Everglades since the fifties. And, incidentally, I didn't know this was possible, but he really did live *in* the Everglades. He had built a home on stilts that could only be accessed by airboat, unless you're an alligator or a snake, in which case you can pretty much walk or slither right up. He kindly gave us a tour of his place, which was fully furnished with television, bathroom, kitchenette, rifles hanging from the wall, and canned goods for extended stays, though I'll tell you right now that actually spending the night there is not something I will ever, ever, ever do. The mere thought was paralyzing actually.

After seeing Don's "house," we climbed back onto the boat and flew recklessly through open waters that weren't totally open if you count the ten-foot sawgrass looming everywhere you turned. Small waterways, like skinny creeks, wound around the landscape with seemingly no logic or continuity, though at any time Don was liable to yank the control bar, steering us straight into the sawgrass, which felt like the parting of the Red Sea but without the Lord's blessing. As we clipped through the stalks of grass at a good forty miles per hour, I yelled to Scott over the engine something to the effect of, "Are we going to die?" I couldn't understand why there didn't seem to be a risk of running aground or hitting a tree stump or a rock, anything that might suddenly halt the boat and send us flying through the air.

Don needed a smoke break anyhow, so he cut the engine and fielded my question with the most expressionless and monotone voice: "It does happen on occasion, but everyone on the boat just flies off in different directions into the water. It's really not that dangerous." All this spoken while cupping his hand over his cigarette, lighting up for what was probably the ten zillionth time in his life—you'd have to have seen him to know this. I didn't find Don's answer especially satisfactory, but figured if he'd lived this long with the alligators and the tobacco, I'd probably make it through an afternoon outing.

Once I'd settled in my mind that I would never ever spend the night in the Everglades, and that I would rather jump into a lion's den than be ejected from an airboat into alligator-infested waters, my next point of interest was how we would get back. We had been careening aimlessly for hours, everything looking exactly the same for miles, not to mention you can't Google this stuff. The place has no zip codes, street names, highways, at least not any official ones that any civilized person knows about. Again, I took one look at

Don, cigarette slanted out of his mouth, catatonically driving the boat like he was coming home from the grocery store he'd been going to his whole life, and I knew he knew the way. I can't tell you for the life of me how he knew. It was an overgrown maze of water, grass, birds, and reptiles—stunning, but it didn't present distinctive signs or landmarks. No instances of, "Oh yeah, I remember passing that really tall grass earlier."

I suppose he had a sense or a recognition that was several layers thick, like my guitar teacher, Melissa, who hears a song and can immediately tell you that the chord progression has moved from G to A minor to Fmaj7 flat 5, and all I can tell you is that I think I like the melody. I hear the song as a whole, but she hears the intricacies that tell her where it's all going, like Don can spot an old bird's nest and notice where the sun is, which somehow tells him to take a left. They're both lifelong students of signs and arrows, just in vastly different fields.

As Margaret, April, and I drove back to the hotel, we couldn't stop talking about the oddities and treasures of the day. We really felt we had met a master in Don, someone whose expertise was worthy of a weighty tome being written about him; we hated the thought of him eventually passing on and all that knowledge going with him. It made me wonder, not so much if I had a hidden area of genius, but if I had eyes to see like Don. Not so I could maneuver the Everglades, but so I could wade through life with more discernment, with keener vision. I want to spend less time getting lost and hung up; I want to be able to spot the trappings of false gods before being caught in their tendrils. I desire to see what is not obvious, to recognize the signs that flash caution and danger.

o   o   o

The past few years have highlighted a few of these signs that I never saw as road markers before. I realized that many of the emotions and issues I was struggling with had their roots in the idols I had given control to. Things like jealousy, anger, and fear, which I used to view as ultimate problems in themselves, were actually arrows that pointed to far bigger issues, the false gods of my heart. These emotions became the signs I learned to read, the ones that signaled that something was wrong—that my deepest affections had been misplaced. It took a lot of bouts with these undesirable feelings and emotions for me to finally discover that they actually had their roots in the gods I was depending on.

I remember when I first arrived in Nashville and the record I had released was failing miserably. My record company couldn't get radio to add any of my singles for anything, while the songs of other new artists were spinning across the airwaves, repeating like broken records. Whenever I heard their songs or discovered news of their success, I'm ashamed to say my blood pumped with extra force, driving an aching pain into the pit of my stomach. Though I never spoke it or even admitted it to myself, I rued their achievement. I was jealous and hurting that my own songs weren't being heard and received with such explosive excitement.

Though it took me awhile to understand, this envy and subtle anger was not something I could merely turn off apart from first dealing with the idol of my heart—personal success. Though it was not wrong or unreasonable for me to desire that my work prosper, the problem lay in the fact that it had become, as Tim Keller puts it, an ultimate thing. In my mind, it was the key to all things good and satisfying. And because this is Christ's sole position, this belief did not go over so well, about as well as the Israelites looking to a golden calf.

During the demise of my record, I experienced almost no joy. I was completely undone by something that was indeed difficult but should not have been devastating. It wasn't until the Lord and I undertook the long journey of dealing with this heart-idol that my jealousy and anger began to melt away. Though this wasn't a quick process, as I learned to discover my worth and identity as they related to Christ and not simply in what I could put my hand to, my idol of achievement became dismantled. Eventually envy imperceptibly gave way to a new place of being able to revel in others' achievements, peaceful that God was as present in my own life even when my successes didn't look the same.

Now, when feelings of jealousy or anxiousness overwhelm me, if I'm at all in tune, I try to step back and see where they are leading. What is it that I desire so intently that is being threatened? Which of my functional gods is being compromised to the point of causing me this much stress? Why do I feel so inordinately strongly about something? What is the object of my affection filling in me that should be coming from God?

Just writing about this conjures up old feelings and seasons that were simply miserable because my affections were misguided as I looked to people and things to deliver contentment and happiness. When someone else threatened those things, it triggered a jealousy that could only be cooled by the tearing down of the idol. It made little sense to deal with the jealousy without first dealing with the false god, given that the one fueled the other.

James details this further: "What causes fights and quarrels among you? Don't they come from your desires that battle within you? You want something but don't get it. You kill and covet, but you cannot have what you want. You quarrel and fight. You do not have, because you do not ask God. When you ask, you do not receive, because you ask with wrong motives, that you may spend what you get on your pleasures" (James 4:1–3). James is saying that the reason behind the fighting and jealousy among us is that we can't get the things we think we need to be content. When someone else is standing in the way of those things, excessive bitterness and anger arise inside us. We become consumed by the need to salvage what is being taken away, especially if that thing is meeting a significant need in us.

My dad has always been such a great example of someone who rarely gets blindsided by jealousy. He's never one to fight over things or money or status, he doesn't meticulously guard his ego, he's happy for those who have more than him, even if it's been obtained unjustly. He just doesn't get ruffled about things or threatening people, and it's not because he's easygoing or dispassionate. It's because most everything he needs or wants he finds in God and his ability to provide. Though not perfect, he implicitly trusts God in so many areas of his life that there's not a lot that can be threatened, meaning there's little source for jealousy. In essence, there just aren't a lot of idols lying around in his heart.

o o o

I've spoken on the topic of no other gods a few different times, the last time to a small gathering in the mountains of Colorado. One woman in the group who was deeply troubled pulled me aside after one of the sessions. I felt for her, as she had placed a lot of needless burdens on herself, mostly in the form of guilt. She said that she felt the need to confess her idol of fear to me, hoping to be set free from its stifling cloak. I had to sit back for a moment and carefully ponder my next statement, as I didn't think fear was her idol as much as it might point to one. I told her that I tended to view fear more like the guard that stands outside the gate of an idol; it's the thing that keeps us closely attached to a god. She looked at me slightly puzzled, certain that her fear was indeed the only offender, the idol itself.

After hearing the sensitive nature of her story, I remained steadfast in my thinking. Not that it was my place anyway, but I just couldn't attribute a false god to her fear, though I definitely saw a few behind it that led to her anxiety. Because she had been a child of abuse and abandonment, her situation was far more complex than anything I could offer at the moment, though no doubt her painful past had led to her hyperfearfulness. She needed someone with a more fitting skill set than my own to address the deeper issues of her heart, yet I believe the principle remained: It wouldn't have done her any good to renounce her so-called god of fear without having first dealt with whatever gods lay beneath the surface.

Fear has presented itself as a monster in my life, the kind that lies beneath the bed in the dark, ready to pounce at any moment. Since fright can easily get stirred up in the confines of my mind, I must often ask the questions "What is fueling this?" or "Where is this coming from?" If we're honest with ourselves, fear can point to the god of money or success, the desire for exclusive relationships, people, and so on. We might lose sleep over our finances, terrified that if the continued bounty of income is threatened, it may interfere with a lifestyle that has become synonymous with our happiness. This is nothing more than the god of materialism.

I remember a woman who used to fret and fear over the potential of someone more beautiful or talented moving onto her street or into her workplace. I saw her go to astounding lengths to avoid beautiful women, even to the point of not going to certain functions or parties, simply because "she" was going to be there. The friends who I've watched navigate through this debilitating and complicated lifestyle live in constant fear of losing their beauty or achievement-oriented status, yet the root of the problem has little to do with fear and everything to do with the false gods of image, success, and outward beauty.

Much like jealousy, fear is a great sign pointing toward who or what we are placing our hope in. The same goes for anger. Anytime we feel the volcanic rise of anger, it's vital to stop and ask the questions, "What's being threatened here?" "What am I afraid I am going to lose?" "What goal of mine is being blocked?" "What's so important that is causing me to explode or lose control?" Strong emotions like any of these are excellent reasons to look where the emotion is pointing. It doesn't mean that a false god is always lurking, but it can mean that, and I've found it essential to trace these overwhelming feelings and reactions back to their source.

This process has been extremely helpful in identifying the functional gods that often lie subtly beneath the surface. Because the onslaught of idols is so overwhelmingly present, it's easy to miss our reliance upon them. It's why I've made it a practice to ask the Lord to help me follow my unruly emotions to someone or something I might have made into an ultimate thing. Inordinate fear, anger, bitterness, jealousy, envy, sadness, and so on have been telling signs that have often led me straight to the far bigger issues of my life—the idols of my heart. If only I got to wear the cool headphones for this.

# (11)

# THERE

Tracing our emotions and fears and plain sin back to the idols of our hearts is an essential practice. It does us little good to believe in the concept of turning from our false gods if we have no idea how to get to them in the first place, or worse yet, whether or not we even have any. Once we've learned to follow the outcroppings of our unruly emotions to our functional gods, once we're standing at their feet, there's yet another step: moving past our idols and into the presence of God. All of this requires not just a turn from, but a turn to.

As we saw before, it is not just a turn to God, but to *our* God, the One who gave his Son so we might have relationship with him. We've seen many obstacles that hinder this turning: pain, the deception of idols, debilitating fear of what we might lose, and a continual lust for more. And yet still there are other things that preclude us from entering into a sweet and intimate relationship with God.

One of those blockages is our inability to sense his presence at different bends in our lives. We go through difficulties or unexplained tragedies or enduring seasons of low-grade pain or mere silence, wondering if the Lord has forgotten us, or if he's chosen to look elsewhere. We panic and turn to whatever we can get our hands on, unaware that all the while God is closer than our breath. The knowledge of the "there-ness" of God, regardless of how it sometimes feels, is essential as we turn from the lesser things that deceptively seem there, and turn to the One who is there. Remember the practices of prayer, community, and Scripture meditation in the chapter called "loved less," as these will breathe life into the process.

o   o   o

I remember sitting on the couch with my mom, a little anxious over something that used to overtake me as a kid: the security of my salvation. Though now far removed, it's a feeling I can well capture, as ultimate abandonment by God was a significant fear I tried to shake while growing up. Knowing that the truths of Scripture would be a balm for my fears, my mom suggested we do a Bible study together, praying that the Holy Spirit would witness to my own of his presence. I think I was about twelve the day I sat next to her with a big Bible draped across my lap, one that drove me deeper into the cushions. I was a fearful little thing, my mind always twirling about tornadoes and robbers and demons and something terrible happening to my parents. Bad dreams. I'm not sure where all this came from, but fear was a mighty wrestler that pinned me to the mat countless times.

Even at a very early age I knew that God was the only One for whom fear was no match, but I had difficulty unlocking that power. The seemingly elusive combination lay bound up in something as simple but difficult as sensing his presence, his nearness. My staggering fears propelled me to pursue God early, desiring to hear him drive away my fears. In some circumstances this was instantaneous: a verse, or a comforting word that I could take hold of, delivering me from whatever was making me so afraid. But mostly this issue of trust and closeness to God has proven to be a process. I fear less as I grow in my relationship with God, but so much of this takes time as intimacy blossoms through the sweet and the precarious bends of life.

As I sat on the couch next to my mom, she asked me something that to this day shows the class and wisdom I so admire about her. "Kelly, what's one word you would use to describe God?" I don't know how long I mulled over the question, though it would have been unlike me to have thrown something out off the cuff—I didn't want to get this one wrong. Not that my mom was looking for a correct answer but for a window into how my twelve-year-old heart was glimpsing the Lord. I gave her such a view by answering with the word *mysterious*.

I looked up at my mom for backup, for support, as if I desperately wanted that to be her word too. "Mom, wouldn't you say God is mysterious? Isn't that your word?"

I called my mom about this incident the other day, wondering what she remembered of our conversation. She responded with decorative detail, telling me it was one of the more prominent memories she has of my childhood. She sadly recalled being torn between wanting to support me in my answer and wanting to be honest in her own description. *Mysterious* was not her word. It wasn't her second or tenth or even fiftieth. She experienced God as close, comforting, attainable, loving, warm. Of course she agreed that the omnipotent God was mysterious on some level—for as God, he is beyond finding out—but mysterious was not at all how she experienced her Savior.

As she weighed her response to me, I remember trying to tame my quivering voice and quell my tearing eyes. My childlike intuition sensed she was going to say something very different from my description, but I deeply wanted someone—my mom of all people—to pick my word, to tell me that she experienced God as mysterious too. I didn't want to be the only one, especially since I longed to know him more intimately.

Though it pained her, my mom didn't change her word. She looked into my anxious and tearful eyes and simply said, *"There.* He is *there."*

God being there was pretty much the exact opposite of mysterious, at least in the way I meant it—elusive, unreachable, a little inconsistent. "But, Mom, don't you think he's also mysterious?" I pleaded. I remember her looking at me lovingly but gently shaking her head. She recently told me how afraid she was of crushing me with her answer, yet she wanted to tell me her genuine experience of

God. She desperately wanted me to feel at rest but didn't want to slough the whole thing off by not relaying her honest feelings or by throwing "*mysterious*" out simply to make me feel better. It's one of those conversations that neither of us has forgotten, one that's stuck with my mom with even greater poignancy as she longed for her child to be able to rest in her Savior's arms.

I'm not sure what word I would use to describe God today, but *mysterious* would be well down the list. Again, not because he isn't far beyond my ability to grasp, but because he has equally revealed himself to me. I think of the apostle Paul who spoke to the Athenians on Mars Hill about their false objects of worship along with an altar with the inscription "To an Unknown God." He took the coveted opportunity to tell them that the God they viewed as unknown was actually quite knowable, indeed "he is not far from any one of us."

As we make our way forward into a closer relationship with Christ, we must revisit the truth that he is not just God, but our God, and in order for us to experience him as ours, we must trust he is there.

o   o   o

As I continued to work through my fears as a child and into my more grown-up years—and doggone it, right now—I reveled in truths such as, he is not far from any one of us. I cherished the idea of God being close to me; it has been my stay. I also clung to David's writings like Psalm 34:18, "The LORD is close to the brokenhearted." I would hold verses like this up to my chest at night, clutching their pages before falling asleep beneath their comfort, their threads of truth blanketing me in security. These Scriptures became my anchor in tumultuous seas of hurt and disappointment, settling me amid the tossing.

I loved prayer verses, such as Psalm 17:8: "Keep me as the apple of your eye; hide me in the shadow of your wings," and Psalm 119:117: "Uphold me, and I will be delivered." I would pray these and myriad others, longing to experience the nearness and assurance of God's presence.

I know this is the cry of many hearts, as so many get swallowed up in tragedy, hardship, or life's monotony, which often drown God's voice and presence. I know of people, and have experienced seasons myself, who pray and read Scripture seemingly to no avail. Yet even our experiences cannot trump the truth and beauty of the living, breathing Bible, nor of Christ our Great High Priest. Hebrews 4:15–16 says, "For we do not have a high priest who is unable to sympathize with our weaknesses.... Let us then approach the throne of grace with confidence, so that we may receive mercy and find grace to help us in our time of need." Christ is not mystified by our weakness, our fear that perhaps he is not with us, our wonderings about his love. He became one of us for many reasons, one being his ability to sympathize with our humanity. Being able to approach him with this understanding has greatly helped my sense of his there-ness in my life.

Each of these verses, and a host more, represents a specific story for me—many of them several, as I revisit their words in different seasons of life. They have become interwoven into the seam of my experiences, threads that have hemmed me into an intimacy with the Father who is more there than I have ever known. And this is especially important as it relates to the false gods we place our hope in, as they often present themselves as being steady and reliable, providing a presence that can feel close and consistent, even if betraying at the same time. Being present is one of their strongest hooks.

And isn't the simple presence of someone or something what we so desperately crave? I think of the common phrases "I will always be there for you" and "That person was always there for me." It's the "there" and the "always" that are the selling points, the glorious marriage of not only getting someone who is there, but someone who will always be there. After many stabs at this I found out—probably a hundred years after everyone else—that this is actually impossible when it comes to people or things. No matter how virtuous or overflowing with integrity and love a friend or spouse may be, no person can possibly always be there for you. This is a place reserved solely for God, a position that only he is capable of, though our experience of his presence is not nearly as consistent as the reality of it.

When I have difficulty sensing him, I am far more prone to start banging down the door for a good false god. I find this with others as well. I talk to so many people who say they can't sense God's presence, or that he feels distant or removed, or that they feel they've disappointed him, or that he's left them in a sea of pain they can't swim out of. I, too, have woven in and out of these times, as recently as last week: I was out walking with a friend and told her I was afraid to cry out to God with too much passion for fear that I might not hear anything on the other end. I didn't want to throw my heart on the line in case no relief attended me. Sometimes it feels easier to wait the thing out instead of really pleading with God for an experience of him. Or worse yet, easier to run to a replacement god we can actually get our hands on.

o   o   o

I believe this is what happened to the Israelites while they waited for Moses to return from receiving the Ten Commandments. They became restless and impatient, deciding that a lifeless golden baby cow of all things might suit their leadership fancy a bit better than hanging around a little longer for Moses, whose past accomplishments had been small and unimpressive like parting the Red Sea and stuff. So they actually said the following to Aaron: "Come, make us gods who will go before us. As for this fellow Moses who brought us up out of Egypt, we don't know what has happened to him" (Ex. 32:1). And so we get back to this issue of presence again. The people wanted a present leader through whom they could experience a present God, and even though God had never left them for even a moment, they were willing to turn to the false for something that absolutely couldn't offer anything more than simply being in their midst. It couldn't think, speak, breathe, lead, but darn it if it wasn't just there.

It's the times when God seems distant that are precisely what make our functional gods so appealing, because for the most part we can get to them. They're available. We can dial them up, order them in, grab them out of the fridge, manipulate them to come over, or whatever we can think of. We'd rather have the golden calf we can at least stare at and maybe wish into life, as opposed to believing in and standing upon a God we can't always sense.

We're all about the quick fix, like Elaine, my neighborhood crack addict who is constantly in and out of jail, occasionally showing up at different homes looking for a sandwich or flip-flops or a buck to ride the bus. Two of my friends tended to her on a regular basis, making her peanut-butter and jelly sandwiches, taking her to the grocery store, and just plain talking to her like a human being. One day they accidentally left their keys in the door, which was a timely accident for Elaine who happened to be wandering by—when she's in need, stealing is not beneath her. She took the keys to their car and stole the ten dollars in change out of the console, but brilliantly left the $35,000 BMW. It was way too much hassle for her to think of trying to sell a car when a few bucks would do the trick for the next fix. Oh, and she kindly left the keys in the mailbox.

And so it went with the Israelites and their golden calf, which in some mysterious way offered a hasty solution. When Moses came down off the mountain, he was holding the Ten Commandments, which the Bible describes in a way that ascribes more value to them than I can comprehend: "The tablets were the work of God; the writing was the writing of God" (Ex. 32:16). It helps me to step back from the scene a bit, as if I were looking on from the mountain's peak: The writings of the one and only God were in Moses' hands as he neared the statue of a calf that was the centerpiece for an Israelite throwdown. Could we go from more supreme to more base in one step? Imagine what they had missed out on, the very work of God in exchange for something that couldn't blink, much less lead them out of the desert.

As a result of their celebration mix-up, the rest of Exodus 32 doesn't go so well. Lots of lives were lost as the Lord had to deal with the unbelief and sheer mayhem of the Israelites. But from my viewpoint, the worst doesn't happen until chapter 33 when the Lord tells Moses to go ahead and take the Israelites into the Promised Land. At first glance this doesn't seem like such a bad deal, like getting ice cream for sassing your mom. "Leave this place … and go up to the land I promised on oath to Abraham, Isaac and Jacob.… I will send an angel before you and drive out the Canaanites, Amorites, Hittites, Perizzites, Hivites and Jebusites. Go up to the land flowing with milk and honey. But I will not go with you, because you are a stiff-necked people and I might destroy you on the way" (33:1–3).

It's the "I will not go with you" part that suddenly becomes the big deal-breaker for me. I'm all about some Promised Land, a little milk and honey, angels knocking some enemies around, but not without God. And if I were to swap out honey and milk for things like my favorite Nashville restaurants, and the Promised Land for the restored cottage I just lost to another buyer, and a protective angel for a lifelong companion, my stance would remain unchanged—I don't want it without the Lord's presence.

Incidentally, life without God—even apparent blissful life—was not an option for Moses. Exodus 33:15 quotes him as saying, "If your Presence does not go with us, do not send us up from here." He found nothing alluring about even what was sworn to his forefathers, Abraham, Isaac, and Jacob—the coveted land of Canaan they were all aspiring to and wandering around in the desert for—if God was not going with them. Without the "there" factor, all bets were off.

In God's great mercy he said to Moses, "I will do the very thing you have asked, because I am pleased with you and I know you by name" (33:17). On a side note, we see the beauty of someone who stands in the gap for another, how God kept leading the Israelites who had turned their backs on him because he was pleased with Moses. It reminds me of what Abraham did for Lot, what Job did for his friends, and what Christ did for us, each of them garnering the favor and blessing of God for those they desperately cared for. How we must plead for the ones we love.

I take comfort in this story as it reminds me that God is never removed from our lives despite how we may feel. When I'm experiencing a distance or a silence, I am exhorted to be vigilant against the temptation to chase down an idol. The Israelites were missing their leader for a time, never understanding that the entire departure was for their good. If ever God was present with them it was when he was painstakingly charting out the laws of liberty (the Ten Commandments) that would bring freedom and life to his chosen people. While not comprehending such a blessing, they turned to the jewelry on their necks, tossed it in a fire, and massaged out a golden calf to worship.

As the roots of my relationship with God have spread themselves more broadly, I am discovering the there-ness of God to be not only stable and true, but entirely essential. I do not want to do anything or be anyplace where he is not. I would rather suffer in his presence than live in exhilarating bliss in his absence. The very thing I longed for as a child—his nearness—is one of the most important qualities that separates Christ from all the functional gods who bid for our time, even when we can't feel it. He will never leave us nor forsake us.

How sweet to discover him as my mom knows him—as simply there. I wouldn't trade it for anything, not even for mysterious.

# (12)

# TRUST

After finishing the writing process for the Living Room Series curriculum, *No Other Gods,* I assumed writing a book on the same topic would be breezy. I was sort of hoping to be able to write it while doing things, like napping. It seemed since most of the legwork had been expended over the two years (on and off) it had taken me to write the Bible study, I would have little more to do than put the concepts into book prose. How hard could this be? I wondered. I don't know why I still pose questions like this to myself, because it's always hard! Everything's hard. It's like when you're asking for directions and someone says you can't miss it, which has now become my cue to allow an extra twenty minutes. Things just aren't ever as easy as I imagine, and taking this topic of modern-day idols and writing it into a book has proven no different.

After weeks of a lot of staring and deleting, writing some more, then erasing as much as I wrote, I couldn't place my finger on the culprit behind my writer's block. It wasn't as if I were unfamiliar with the subject, yet it felt like trying to knead dough with a wooden spoon—nothing was coming easy. I realized that in many ways the curriculum I had written was God's story played out in the lives of characters in the Bible, but much of this book was God's story played out in my life. This put a personal spin on things that churned with some pain and hard memories. It has not been easy accessing those places and dissecting them through the motions of blotting ink on paper.

Although I grasped the difficult nature of writing a personal book—albeit well into the game—God began to reveal another obstacle, one that I didn't see coming: an issue of trust. I realized as recently as a couple of nights ago I had been withholding from God the fearful experiences I had as a child, the things that made me sit with my mom, reading verses one by one, longing to find something that would still my terror. And questioning the security of my salvation was only one of the ways my fears manifested themselves. I also battled anxiety and depression on and off from somewhere around the age of seven all the way into my twenties. I am thankful that my body and mind found refuge above these waters often for years at a time, but these spans of darkness still added up to some traumatic years for me. My anxiety, and its flipside of depression, was something that at its worst kept me from being able to do the things I normally enjoyed while not in that state—spending the night at friends', going out to eat, playing outside, being part of fun things that no longer seemed fun. Losing my capacity for fun only added to the spiral of hopelessness. When I became older, I even had to drop out of college for a semester, simply unable to sustain the strength and concentration needed to get out and interact, much less study.

When I was little, I prayed throughout the day and every night that God would make me feel better, that I would know he loved me. Though I am so grateful I could actually sleep at night, when I woke in the morning it was as if I was afforded one second of peace until I remembered everything I was experiencing and all of the depression and anxiety crawled on top of me again. The fight began. I toppled over and under my thoughts all day long, back and forth like grappling wrestlers who had endless sources of energy, never seeming to tire though I fought them with all I had.

Because I began experiencing anxiety and depression at such a young age, I had no language for it. I had no words at my disposal to describe what I was going through. No commercials, magazine ads, or the endless talk you hear on the subject today. I had never met or heard of anyone who dealt with what was plaguing me; I only knew how different I felt from my friends who laughed and played, skipping off from their mothers like it never crossed their minds she might not be there when they got back or that something bad might separate the two of them. If I ever mustered the courage to broach what I was feeling with a friend, I only came away feeling more paralyzed, as no one seemed to understand, or simply told me not to worry.

Just last week I was at the movies watching a Pixar animation that I'm sure will be added to their list of hits. I had never thought about it before, but almost every classic kid movie separates the main, vulnerable character from his loved ones as its central theme. Think *Lion King, Toy Story, Finding Nemo, Bambi, Pinocchio* to name just a smattering. This movie was no different as the protagonist got separated from his family in a rush of pandemonium. Panic stricken, he was whisked away by rushing waters, eyes darting every which way, wailing out the names of his dad and his brother to no avail. The theater's silence was broken by the trembling voice of a young boy who yelled out, "Mommy, I don't like this!" I could relate. Thankfully, not so much today, but my heart resonated with his, sort of wishing I could awkwardly force my way down the row so I could hold him for a minute and cover his eyes until all was happily ever after.

Occasionally little things like being at the movies, or taking a walk, or playing with a child will oddly remind me of what I went through in my younger years. Of course, my experiences progressed as I grew up, my fears simply becoming more adult in nature. I am deeply thankful that as I was able to talk about them more, and as my parents progressively understood, they were able to get me the help I needed through a few different avenues. They are both so wonderful, and I am forever thankful that they always did absolutely whatever it took to help me. If ever they fell short, it was only a matter of ignorance and never neglect.

But what about God? The One who is never ignorant, the One who seemingly stood by as I trembled with fear, the One who could have made it all go away with less than a blink? Though I have worked through countless layers of these struggles with him, I had never realized until right in the middle of this book the pieces I have been withholding from him. It's as if I can implicitly trust him for finances, relationships, singleness, career choices, family members, but the mental anguish I wove in and out of from childhood into my early twenties seems off-limits.

In my speaking, worship leading, and writing, I could present him as able, loving, and redemptive in all areas except for my depression and anxiety. Ultimately I felt like God had abandoned me in those times of mental torture, so I quietly and almost unknowingly tucked those memories into the "I'm on my own" corner, thinking that if I never had to revisit that area again, I could sort of let God off the hook and we could both just never mention it. I wasn't expecting God after all these years—in the super-inconvenient time of writing this book, I might add—to lead me to those memories, revealing the places where I didn't trust him.

○    ○    ○

All of this buoyed to the surface for me during a three-week period of a wrenched back and a respiratory illness. As my friend Paige put it, "Back pain is especially hard, because everywhere you go, there you are with your back." Essentially it wasn't all that big of a deal, but with every uncontrollable cough came a tighter lower back, and with every uncomfortable night's sleep on the floor came a more inflamed infection. As the two fed one another I became more depleted, not to mention the stress of being unable to get to all the work that was piling up like snow on every free surface of my house.

For whatever reason, the culmination of sickness, a twisted back, and the pressure of slipping behind started to tug on my mental and emotional reserve. One evening I felt myself begin to ever so slightly slide into that place of despair. Even though I knew my circumstances were fabulously temporary and that on a core level there was nothing seriously wrong, I felt assaulted by old feelings, fears, and a hollowness that concerned me. I started scurrying for the brakes, anything to halt the downward spiral that had hardly even begun. Previously anxious and depressed people don't fiddle around with even the slightest hint in that direction.

I suddenly felt on my own, as if to say since God had seemingly "abandoned" me before in this place, what would keep him from doing it again? At an almost subconscious level, I kept thinking I would have to pull myself up by my own resources. Thankfully, this independent striving was short-lived, as the Lord kindly drew what was beneath the surface to the fully conscious. It occurred to me that I did not trust God with my mind, my sense of well-being.

As the realization slowly took dimension, I lay on my bed with eyes brimming with tears, sad for all those horrendous experiences, and sad that I had withheld them from God. Yet in the midst of my grief, I felt a quiet joy in discovering that he wanted in. I felt like someone was delicately tapping me on the shoulder, as if to say, "Hey, don't leave me out of this."

I am on a journey with the Lord here. I haven't made sense of my own pain, nor am I doubt-free. I may not ever fully know what to make of all that I went through, but I know the Lord wants to enter into what I've been withholding from him. He desires my trust. Though I have grown close to him on so many levels, I now realize that when it came to my mind and my sense of well-being, I have felt on my own at times. I don't want this to be the case any longer, as I desire for him to have all of me. I want to be reconciled to him across the board, not holding back any area where I doubt him as faithful. Even my past memories of panic and depression I desire him to restore so that I can know him as loving, loyal, and present—all the things he cannot help but be, even when I can't understand.

o   o   o

Right in the middle of working through this area of trust I found out that a sweet friend of mine's ten-year-old son was having similar fears and doubts that were keeping him up at night and impeding his day. A normally carefree and independent child, he now struggled to be away from his mom for even an hour at a time. Because I felt so well acquainted with his journey, I told him that he could call or e-mail me anytime if he needed to talk. The other day a message popped up in my mailbox with the subject title FEAR. I took one look at it and thought, *No, Lord. Not today. If this sweet little boy is having a hard time and is writing to tell me about it, I can't take it. It's too close to home. Why aren't you there for him?* When I clicked on his message, it read, "Hey Kelly, its Brian. Yesterday my mom got back from the farm, and I stayed home and I did not get scared. In fact it was as if God had placed an invizable wall between me and fear. And I also turned the light off too." It was the "z" in invizable that really got me.

Touché.

I smiled and was thankful to the Lord for using my ten-year-old buddy to encourage me. He didn't know that his own comfort from the Lord was a timely blessing for me, salve for the memories I haven't quite known what to do with. It was healing, as Brian's intent pursuit of Christ at such a young age reminded me of my own. Though painful and debilitating at times, such battles with fear have caused us both to seek our Savior in perhaps ways the unencumbered ten-year-old may not realize the need for.

(I have to make a quick note here for the person who is struggling or has struggled with acute anxiety or depression. Please do not succumb to the idea that God is punishing you so you will be close to him. Though a closer relationship with him can often be part of the outcome of our pain, this thinking can compound the suffering you are already in. Remember, the Lord is not cruel. As well, he is a healer. Take the necessary measures to get the help you need as you would for any other struggle or hardship. The Lord has profoundly used the expertise of wise mentors, medical doctors, professional godly counselors, and the resources they prescribe to bring health to my body and mind. I praise him for this.)

o   o   o

At a young age, I remember drinking from the pages of Scripture Boaz's description of Ruth and her Savior: "May you be richly rewarded by the LORD, the God of Israel, under whose wings you have come to take refuge" (Ruth 2:12). It was not the mysterious God beneath whose wings Ruth had found shelter, but the "there" God. The God of Israel, who incidentally was not Ruth's heritage. Ruth was a Moabite, from a country considered well outside the chosen people of Israel, spiritually speaking. Yet she followed her mother-in-law, Naomi, back to Bethlehem, embracing not only Naomi's land but her God. Truly he is near even to the seemingly distant or outsider. And truly he was worthy of Ruth's trust, as she left her familiar home, people, and country in exchange for the wings under which she had come to trust him.

I also think of verses like Psalm 20:7: "Some trust in chariots and some in horses, but we trust in the name of the LORD our God." It's a verse that has brought me comfort and instruction when friends, career, and circumstances have failed me. When I have failed myself. How lovely to know that God is stronger, greater, nobler than the robust horses and gleaming chariots that brought victory for ancient warriors. He is more worthy of trust than any person, nation, or false god in which we place our hope. I have had to learn this by experience, choosing to trust him in places and situations that struck fear or sadness or grief into my heart.

And, incidentally, choosing to trust hasn't been as easy as flipping a switch or snapping my fingers. It's been more like chaining myself to a tree during a hurricane, whatever I can do to stay the course. I remember one evening when I knew the Lord had told me to decline an invitation to a gathering that was bound to cause me hardship, a situation that would perfectly pull on everything fleshly. The only problem with missing the function was that it meant being at home by myself. I realize that there is greater suffering in the world than being home alone on a Friday night, but I'll tell you that keeping myself in my house that night took every ounce of physical and spiritual energy as I resisted what felt like a magnetic, superhuman pull from across town. I combated terrible thoughts of loneliness, angst, fear, all sorts of things that raged seemingly out of nowhere. The decision to trust was quick, but the walking out of it was a night of ordeal.

o   o   o

As part of growing my trust, I also read about Hagar in Genesis 16, who fled from her mistress, Sarah. She was alone and abandoned, suffering in the desert while pregnant, when the angel of the Lord found her and said, "Hagar, servant of Sarai, where have you come from, and where are you going?" He inquired about her life. He told her that she would have a son. Perhaps most importantly to her, he called her by name. This elicited a worshipful reciprocation as Hagar then called him by name, a new name: El Roi, which means, "You are the God who sees me."

Even at an early age, I took comfort that God was the One who sees. The One who saw me. I began to grow in my relationship with not only the mysterious God—the One past finding out—but El Roi, the One who is intimately acquainted with the details of my life, who cares closely, as opposed to distantly preoccupied from afar. The One who sees.

Looking back I'm not sure I would have sought him the way I did had it not been for my deep struggles with anxiety and depression. They were the spark that sent me running to his Word, scouring his truths for what would put me at rest. I dug deep, mining for what was well beneath the surface. Like what is recorded in Isaiah 45:3: "I will give you the treasures of darkness, riches stored in secret places, so that you may know that I am the LORD, the God of Israel, who summons you by name." The Lord is still past finding out, still shrouded in mystery for sure, but it is the "there" God who has called me by name, who has called Brian, who has called you.

You may have your own corner of life's pain that you've been withholding from the Lord. You may have decided a long time ago that he let you down and in that particular area you're simply on your own. Maybe you can trust him with your marriage but not your finances; you can look to him for your health but not your children; your career, but not your personal relationships. I pray that whatever you've decided you can't trust him with, you will offer up. I hope you will take down the no-trespassing sign, that you will invite him into what only he can heal.

Though I can't make perfect sense of it all—any more than Ruth could make sense of losing her husband and following her mother-in-law back to a foreign land, all the while weeping—surely the beauty of coming to trust him under his everlasting wings is worth more than what I can't understand.

## (13)

# ANTI-LEGALISM

I would be remiss if suddenly you felt overwhelmed by the onslaught of idols, surprised by their insidious deception, guilt-ridden by your dependence upon them—all without a remedy. We've defined them as anything that is inflated to take the position of God in our lives, any-one or anything that becomes an ultimate thing. We've discovered that some of their roots trace back to experiences of being unloved, rejected, abused—or the flipside, of having it all while ironically having an insatiable desire for more. We've identified a few of their more prominent characteristics, which revolve around subtle deceit, blatant lies, and flashy seduction. But how do we rid our hearts of them? Because how not to do something can be equally as important as how to do it, I thought it would be worth giving a little time to the "how not to" way.

Legalism. I wrote about it in my first book, *Water Into Wine,* and the companion Bible study to this book, The Living Room Series: *No Other Gods*. It is worth touching on again, simply because it is a truly dreadful form of misery to move and breathe under. And if we want to turn away from false gods, being motivated by legalism will put anyone on the fast track to burnout and raging frustration. I've never seen a person successfully function under it long-term. I've seen some people go fifteen, twenty years, but have eventually and regretfully watched them explode out of a skin so tightly wrapped that they went from considering jazz music satanic to gobbling up pornography as fast as they could find it.

No one can do the righteousness thing on their own, because righteousness cannot be manufactured by outward behaviors. This puts the average Christian in a bit of a bind, because most of us desire righteousness but think that accomplishing it means doing a little more of this and a little less of that. If we carry this mentality over to ridding ourselves of false gods, we will become rule oriented, which will either lead to self-righteousness or self-defeat. Neither has ever worked well for me.

o    o    o

Yesterday I flew to Virginia to meet someone whose birth has changed my life. She is eighteen hours old, a little fatigued, and still settling onto the earth. When she's awake, her eyes dart around as if she's inspecting the world, deciding whether or not this will all do for her. She's a life-changing little thing because she's the first child to be born to any of my siblings, officially making me Aunt Kelly. Favorite Cool

Aunt Kelly from Nashville is what I'm ultimately reaching for, but I'll keep you posted.

When Maryn entered the world, my entire family including my brother's fiancée was piled up against the door, my mom and dad ready to beat it down with an ax, as this now meant grandparent status for them. I was in Nashville rolling out pizza dough at a friend's house when my mom called to hold up her phone to the outside of the hospital room door so I could hear my first niece squawking a thousand miles away. "Maryn's here!" she proclaimed teary-eyed.

A few minutes later the family was given entrance, my poor sister, Katie, intruded upon in ways I'd rather not imagine as an entire group of out-of-their-minds family members descended upon her room and grasped at that poor baby. As if the whole entering-the-world-through-something-as-void-of-delight-as-a-birth-canal weren't enough, Maryn arrived to flash photography, hoots, and hollers, like a celebrity emerging from her limo. She's a star!

A week before Katie delivered, I called to check in on her and her protruding self. I was curious to see how she was doing, what she was feeling, and how many things she had knocked over with her stomach. She said she was pretty much just hanging around, waiting for her entire life to change. She asked me when I thought I'd come home to see the baby, and I told her I'd try to get there within a few weeks of Maryn's birth, knowing I had a lot of travel for work. Two days later when Maryn was born, the oddest sensation overcame me. Between making those pizzas and my phone sounding off every few seconds with another picture mail of my new little girl, I suddenly had to go.

Right then. There was no way I could wait. Work could be tabled, flights rerouted, and the credit card charged a few more times. The next morning I was off. If ever there was license for spontaneity, Maryn was it.

Now I know this kind of thing happens every day all over the world, but I'm telling you, Maryn is one of the most miraculous things I have ever experienced. I spent hours holding her, just staring. "Quick, she's yawning! You missed it, everyone; she just sneezed!" Something about her perfectly and intricately formed ears was just mesmerizing to me. But perhaps more than anything else, I was delighted at the notion that she is me, us, a Minter. And just by virtue of her existence, she has made me an aunt. I can do nothing to become an un-aunt. I did nothing to become one—Katie kind of shouldered that one for me. I was rolling out pizza dough, for heaven's sake, while she was in labor, which is really a great deal come to think of it.

Even though I didn't have to work for this status, I want to be great at acting like what I already am—an aunt. I'm not working for the title, but because of it. I've bought her cute clothes from Georgetown, have flown up to see her, will bring her to Nashville when she's old enough. I don't do these things to become an aunt; I do them because I am one.

In the same way, we do not turn from our false gods to become God's children. We turn from them because we are. In Romans 6:11, Paul says we are to count ourselves dead to sin and alive to Christ. I love the King James Version, which uses the word *reckon*. We reckon ourselves alive to God, because we are alive to him. And we reckon ourselves dead to sin, because we are dead to sin. Our choices, behavior, and actions are an outflow of our status as children of God. When we get it the other way around—doing in order to gain status—we become fatigued and frustrated.

o　o　o

One of the reasons this issue of legalism continually surfaces for me is because I've crumbled under it while sincerely striving to do the "right thing." When I was growing up, I was taught at my Christian school that in order to be a good Christian you had to do good things and not do bad things. Though not exactly stated, the underlying message was that we have the power to make good Christians out of ourselves. Sort of like if we eat enough pasta and use our hands a little more we might have a shot at becoming Italian.

Because I have always been a little on the uptight, intense, and high-strung side—I actually think I'm quite relaxed, but this is what I hear—I was very serious about securing good Christian status. I didn't consider the Bible a book of mere suggestions, but viewed it soberly as God-inspired. When I read prescriptive verses like "Be holy, for I am holy," I took them literally, the way I still believe they are to be taken.

If it hadn't been for this off-putting thing called my flesh, I think my chances for success would have been quite high actually. It has always gotten in the way of my good intentions and some really good holiness. If there were a simple way to get rid of my flesh, righteousness would be an immediate and lovely reality for me. The problem is that my flesh has to die—not my actual physical skin and tissue, but the nasty core of me that selfishly craves, gossips, covets, steals, lies, lusts, envies, hates. It's human nature left to itself. It's tempting to think that I can squelch and manage this nature as I mature, but the harsh reality is that my flesh must die not so much because of what it does, but because of what it is (Ps. 51:5).

The book of Romans talks a lot about this, as Paul tells us that when we entered into relationship with Jesus, when we trusted him for forgiveness and heaven and salvation, our flesh was put to death when Christ was put to death. He says that now that Christ is resurrected, we, too, have new life and are led by the Holy Spirit, not by the written code of the law. It's no longer about doing this and not doing that so we can be acceptable to God, but about "that" being put to death so we are now free to live for "this." And if this is all entirely too complicated, I have a story from kindergarten.

○  ○  ○

I grew up in a couple of Christian schools where legalism was prevalent. I remember being peeled off my mom's neck at the mature age of four on the front stoop of my Christian preschool. My fun-filled days were comprised mostly of Bible lessons, Scripture memorization classes, and math. We had coloring breaks, but staying inside the lines was strongly enforced, so I grew up to be a rather nervous colorer. My teacher, Mrs. Dodgers, was a heavyset woman in her early sixties who walked around with a warm and engaging scowl. Behind her desk, where most teachers might hang the alphabet in bubble letters with cartoonish bunnies and smiling bears, Mrs. Dodgers decided that two wooden paddles might be more motivating.

This plan worked great by the way. I obeyed all the rules perfectly. I never talked back and was an excellent student. The only problem was that I would come home—to use my mom's exact terminology—madder than a hornet. As a wee little kid I would storm in the house and start wreaking havoc on my mom and siblings. After six hours of trying to hold in all my wayward tendencies, I would explode. Trying to control my outward behavior without anyone reaching my heart was a losing battle.

I never had a relationship with Mrs. Dodgers. I did what she said because I was scared to death of her. Sadly, what she never understood was that her rules could affect my behavior but could never change my heart. Though this isn't an official definition, I think this is pretty much the heart of legalism. It's contrary to the message of the gospel, which says that everyone has fallen short of the glory of God, but because of God's grace we are no longer ruled by the condemning law but have the life of Christ indwelling us. It's the difference between outwardly displaying "goodness" out of duty and having the goodness of Christ flow out of me because he has changed my heart.

I think I always believed that I had trusted Christ for this righteousness, this change of heart. But I think mostly I had trusted him for justification (being pronounced righteous because of what Christ did for me on the cross), but not so much for sanctification (the progressive process of holiness and becoming more like him). Basically, I had trusted Christ for something as big as salvation, but not for daily things like how to deal with this selfish, jealous, anxious nature of mine. I figured that part was up to me.

This is where we can really become burnt out—when we decide that we are in charge of putting this sin nature to death, of dealing with our idols, because the only thing we've got with which to kill our flesh is our flesh. It's why I see so many people frustrated and exhausted by sermons and more Bible studies and more lists of what they can and can't do. It's so defeating when you spend years trying to beat the pulp out of your own flesh with your own flesh.

o    o    o

Right now I'm returning from South Florida, where dramatic fires are burning all over the state from a long season of drought. When I stepped outside this morning, it smelled like the entire neighborhood was having a barbeque, which would have been odd at 8:45 a.m., but goodness knows I'll take a cheeseburger anytime of the day. The whole sky was hazy and the sun's rays were entirely obscured by the smoke, leaving a glowing ball in the sky. Because I had been cooped up in planes and airports, I decided to go running for a little exercise. In retrospect, my workout was probably the equivalent of smoking five packs of cigarettes. I burned three hundred calories but now have lung cancer.

Attempting to manage or handle my fleshly nature with all its longings on my own is right up there with exercising in contaminated air. It's the ultimate in counter-productivity. That's why it's so important to approach having no other gods before God in a manner that is Holy Spirit empowered.

This is where obedience enters. I equally embrace and eschew obedience depending on the day. The difference between true obedience and legalism is that God empowers us to obey. In Philippians 2:13, Paul says, "For it is God who works in you to will and to act according to his good purpose." So if God has asked something of you, he will enable you to do it—no matter how daunting the task—if you stay humble and close to him. Legalism is when we try to obtain the result of obedience by our own means and strength. It is self-righteousness, as opposed to God's righteousness covering us, and the two are as different as spirit and flesh.

o   o   o

In Galatians, Paul uses the lives of Hagar and Sarah to depict this concept in a way that breathes life into an otherwise difficult concept. We'll be looking at these women more closely in future chapters, but for now, a quick hello will work. In essence, God promised Abraham that he would bear a son through his wife, Sarah. The only snag was that many years went by before this miracle turned into reality. For decades, Sarah was barren and frustrated. She eventually took matters into her own hands and decided a reasonable solution would be to offer her slave girl Hagar to Abraham, in the hopes of getting a son. (Sarah followed the same custom Rachel used when she offered her slave girl to Jacob in hopes of getting a child and shedding her disgrace.) Sarah's plan succeeded, at least in that Hagar indeed bore a son, Ishmael.

Approximately twelve years after Ishmael's birth, Isaac was born to Sarah just like the Lord had promised. A few thousand years after both sons were born, Paul wrote about the story in an inconceivable light:

> Tell me, you who want to be under the law, are you not aware of what the law says? For it is written that Abraham had two sons, one by the slave woman and the other by the free woman. His son by the slave woman was born in the ordinary way; but his son by the free woman was born as the result of a promise.

> These things may be taken figuratively, for the women represent two covenants. One covenant is from Mount Sinai and bears children who are to be slaves: This is Hagar. Now Hagar stands for Mount Sinai in Arabia and corresponds to the present city of Jerusalem, because she is in slavery with her children. But the Jerusalem that is above is free, and she is our mother.... Now you, brothers, like Isaac, are children of promise. (Gal. 4:21–28)

The very simple version of this—the version that corresponds to our idol-ridding approach—is this: We can try to turn from our false gods by a strategy that relies on us, like forcing Hagar to have a child; or we can rely on the power and promise of God to turn from them, just as God eventually gave a baby to Sarah. In essence, what Paul is saying is that Hagar represents the Old Covenant that the Lord had with the Israelites, which required them to keep the law by their own fortitude. This ultimately failed, as the Israelites could not faithfully live up to its standards. So God sent a Savior, Jesus Christ, to keep the law perfectly for us and to exchange our sin for his righteousness, and God sent the Holy Spirit to empower us to live lives of idol-free holiness.

The New Covenant under Christ reflects the way Sarah conceived Isaac—by God's promise and not by her own manipulative hand through Hagar. Paul goes on to tell the Galatians (and us) that we are not children born of the slave woman (Hagar) but of the free woman (Sarah). The New Covenant through Jesus Christ frees us from having to dismantle our idols through legalism—trying a little harder, sitting through another sermon, and gritting our teeth with a smidge more force. Instead, we can dismantle them only through the life of Jesus Christ inside us.

This, of course, doesn't mean passively sitting around waiting for God to magically level the false gods we've been serving, but it does mean that he will give us the strength to be obedient to him, as whatever the Lord asks of us he will help us accomplish (Phil. 2:13). When we attempt to do this in Hagar fashion, we end up with unruly consequences worse than what lay before.

o   o   o

I have never been more experientially aware of my desperate need to live as a child of promise than I have over the last few years. As I found myself bound by the need to secure affection and approval at the expense of all else, I realized that I couldn't snap myself out of such dependency without the power of Christ. This is the New Covenant that Paul is referring to: No longer do I have to strive by the legalism of Hagar; I can live by the promise of Sarah—the promise that comes through the indwelling life of Christ.

As you read through the book of Galatians, you realize that this is not trite, unrealistic church-talk but is a desperate plea from Paul for us to live like the children we are—children of promise, not products of legalistic striving. So as we begin our foray into the world of "what to do next," it is essential that we don't begin by rule-keeping but by freedom that empowers obedience. Plus, it's just a lot easier this way.

# (14)

# PRAYING HAND

Now that we're clearer about what God doesn't want—legalism—we can look more deeply at what he does want—Spirit-empowered obedience. Personally, I used to get secretly annoyed with some of the rules and commands in Scripture. I would have never broadcasted this in Sunday school, or in my home, or anywhere outside my heart for that matter, mostly because I never found the sentiment acceptable—even to myself. Nevertheless, at gut level, I was often bothered by some of God's laws. And I'm not referring to the legalistic, self-righteous, made-up parameters that we often impose upon ourselves. I'm talking about the genuine ones: refraining from jealousy, preferring others above yourself, seeking God first with your time and resources, denying your flesh, remaining pure when the impure feels better, and so on. I lived out of duty, like when I was a kid memorizing Scripture verses for snack-sized candy bars. As I got older, the duties grew beyond memory verses, and my appetite swelled beyond chocolate. I found it difficult to measure up, and even when I succeeded, the payoff seemed paltry.

And so it went with my idols. Why couldn't I have a few here or there? Why did I have to stick with the ancient commands of the Bible, the ones that seemed so constricting and smothering at times? They felt anything but what John calls them in 1 John 5:3—"not burdensome." Why did they feel like a sack of potatoes I couldn't unload? I believe my negative view of God's commands boiled down to two things really: First, I didn't see what the big problem was with my functional gods, and second, I didn't grasp the profound love behind God's precepts to do away with them.

My perspective has since changed. The angle from which I now view his direction is entirely different, like seeing something familiar for the first time from a mountain peak. You get to see with perspective and in context. Suddenly the object of my gaze, the seemingly arbitrary rules, became part of the greater landscape. I began to see God's commands within the grander milieu of his love, protection, freedom, and desire for me to live more fully. I had to climb a mountain to get this perspective, a mountain wrought with a few good heartaches from some of my choice idols. It's where I discovered that there really are some downsides—putting it mildly—to having gods who aren't God.

∘  ∘  ∘

This enlightenment didn't dawn on me until after I emerged from a season of spiritual numbness. I had slipped into it almost imperceptibly.

My relationship with God lay dull; the sublime had turned muted. The fainter my intimacy with him grew, the more my hunger swelled for something to suffice me. I had the garden of Eden's plenty but couldn't quite seem to get at it. I craved satisfaction but had given up a bit on God being the One to grant it. Although I was full of the knowledge of his all-surpassing satisfaction and love, I think I'd resigned myself to believing it was for the super-spiritual and not really for normal me.

Somewhere near the end of this season of confusion and longing, I read the passage I referenced earlier from 2 Kings 17, the one that initially focused me and my living-room girls on this topic of modern-day idols. I found it to be an accurate commentary on my ailing state. I had never seen anything quite like this in Scripture, this worshipping both God and gods. It reminded me of Matthew 6:24, which says that no one can serve two masters. It is impossible to fully give your heart to God while splitting it down the middle. And yet I was torn, my flesh and spirit warring against one another like two evenly matched wrestlers, neither willing to concede but neither strong enough to win. I knew in principle that the Spirit of God living inside me was stronger than my flesh, but as Paul writes in Romans, the one I serve will ultimately dominate my life.

Though it took a while to get here, I eventually began to realize that my obedience to God had been limited. I, like the people in 2 Kings 17, was worshipping God but serving my idols (verse 41). I also found myself sliding down the slick path that God warned about in verse 35: "When the LORD made a covenant with the Israelites, he commanded them: 'Do not worship any other gods or bow down to them, serve them or sacrifice to them.'" I saw this series of behaviors in my life, from worship to bowing down (not physical, but heart posture-wise) to serving to ultimately sacrificing to them. I loved God and deeply wanted to be active in the things that mattered to him, but there were people and things that were ultimately more important when it came to my choices and decisions. Often, my energies were spent on them. I was living the split life James speaks of in James 1:8, the double-minded soul who is unstable in all her ways.

○   ○   ○

I was reminded of this principle a few weekends ago when I went to Noshville's for a leisurely Saturday breakfast. It's one of Nashville's only authentic New York delis, making it a gem amid many knockoffs. (I love the South, but one thing it just doesn't do is New York.) I had been invited to dine with four kids under the age of four over non-kid-friendly items like syrup, bacon grease, and deep purple jelly. (The fact that I left the house in a white T-shirt is a telling sign that I have no children.) I obliged only because these are the most scrumptious children on the planet, one of them being Mary Holland, who is deliciously tomboy and princess. Just last week I caught her running through the yard in a pink dress and pink cowboy boots, her pink tights streaked with grass stains as if to say, I'm all girl but don't mess with me.

When we got to Noshville's, I strategically positioned myself near Mary Holland, luring her into my lap with crayons and coloring books. This bought me about 3.2 minutes of cuddle time, stroking her hair, kissing the top of her head. I finally lost out to the fancy booster seats that each of her three brothers was in—you really can't pass up a good booster seat when you're three, so I didn't feel too bad losing out to the plastic box. Plus I think my constant squeezes and kisses were starting to wear on her. How nice for her to have her own space with no one tugging or cajoling her. So I strapped Mary Holland in at the end of the table, catty-corner to me, so I could still revel in her cuteness. She calls me "Kally," and it's so endearing that I kind of hover around her like a gnat, waiting for her to call my name or acknowledge me on any level. She's an independent little creature, which equally bugs me and makes me like her even more.

I'm not sure what inspires a mom to take four baby children out to breakfast, but then again I have nothing to go on in the kid department, so I just stand back with wide eyes and sigh things like "Wow" in long whispers. When our meals finally arrived, we got everything as situated as possible with that many little ones. Their mother, who is one of those exceptionally calm and stable individuals—the kind who makes you want to fall at her feet and passionately plea, "Teach me!"— put both her hands together, her voice transcending the restaurant's commotion, and cheerfully said, "Praying hands, everyone!" All the kids placed their elbows on the table with hands flat up against one another, no fingers entangled.

As we began to thank God for our food, I noticed Mary Holland's attention straying toward the bacon on her plate, perhaps along with the syrupy pancakes. Both praying hands were impressively sealed together above the table while her gaze drifted to her sizzling breakfast. It was like child hypnosis. You could almost see the miniature scales reflecting in her deep blue eyes tipping back and forth between keeping the prayer form and inhaling some bacon. Which will it be? The tension mounted until finally the possibility of both praying hands and bacon dawned upon her budding mind. After all, this could be what that other hand is all about.

Mary Holland took her right hand and grasped at her slice of bacon, never moving her other, staunchly dedicated, still-praying hand. She shoved her breakfast into her mouth like it might not be there at amen, managing several handfuls. She dipped each bacon slice into the syrup, adorning it with pancake crumbs, while her one resolute praying hand stood unwavering in the air. This made me want to hold her even more, darn it.

I watched her with such affection, reminded of the times in my life when I had given God partial devotion—one praying hand as opposed to the two he demands. It's back to that split devotion in 2 Kings 17, where the people worshipped God and their idols, and whoever is getting your worship will always get your obedience.

And if there's anything that I've realized over the course of my journey it's that God blesses obedience. But partial obedience doesn't really count. God seems to be very big on total, complete, all-encompassing obedience, which is technically the only kind of obedience there is. The especially good news here is that this is quite different from perfect obedience, which implies total obedience done flawlessly. Perfection is not the issue so much as totality is.

Fully agreeing with God's commands and heeding his Spirit is where I understand the far greater importance to lie.

o   o   o

In my first book, *Water Into Wine*, I wrote about the significance of total obedience at the wedding in Cana in John 2:1–12. The story is famous for being Jesus' first recorded miracle and for being the place where he turned water into wine. The wedding banquet had run out of wine, and Jesus' mother asked him to resolve the dilemma. As part of the remedy, Jesus told the servants at the wedding to fill up six ceremonial jugs with water. Scripture says that they did so, and that they did so to the brim.

This signified the totality of their obedience. Not that any of this is mentioned, but who knows if they spilled along the way or broke any glasses like you always hear shattering at inopportune times in restaurants. A flawless performance is not what mattered, but the complete obedience of filling the jars to the brim, holding nothing back. And this is even more significant when one thinks about the fact that the wedding was out of wine, not water. Could the servants have been thinking something along the lines of *Who's the smart guy who thinks he's helping out with the fun water idea?* I always have to keep in mind that this was not perhaps the most logical move the servants could have made, so their obedience is that much more meaningful.

When looking back at my season of spiritual dullness, I realized that much of it had to do with an area of obedience I was holding back on. The Lord was asking me to change some things in my relationships, desiring to mature me in healthier ways while deepening my dependence upon him. Sometimes in these situations it takes someone from the outside to just zing me one. Often it's with a truth I already know somewhere inside me but have wiggled or reasoned myself out of because it's too painful to contend with. Or it's one I've layered over with so many justifications—like surely God can't mean that, or how's a person supposed to have any fun in life, or the Bible is being a little extreme here. I've found that the longer I go in my rationalizations, the truth that I once believed becomes so anemic that I hardly know it's there. This must be what it means when the Bible talks about quenching the Holy Spirit. You can starve a certain truth for so long that it becomes unrecognizable within you. This is when a zinger is in order.

My friend Barbara, who is a godly counselor in the Washington, D.C., area, agreed to help (or zing) me over the phone. She kindly offered to extend her expertise in my stuck and jaded state. I had no idea what was coming, which is probably why I asked for her assistance. I remember being casually sprawled across my bed, rehearsing the details of my loneliness and stuckness over the phone. (Sometimes figuring out a healthy balance in relationships can mean seasons of loneliness, but praise God, I'm never separated from his presence.) Barbara asked me a few questions; I volleyed with a few answers; sweet little Barbara attacked the net and smashed the ball past me at four hundred thousand miles an hour. And I wasn't even looking for a competition! Just a little help, thank you.

Barbara didn't prescribe any more rounds, or refer me for any shock treatment, incidentally. In my case, it was a simple obedience issue. But in deference to her overhead smash, I wanted her to know all the things I had done and not done in obedience to Christ. I tried to convince her that I had been obedient in many areas and that given all I had gone through, I was actually faring quite well. Surely God could overlook a little stretch here or there. Barbara was gracious but firm in reminding me of that one thing—something I had grown a little fuzzy on, simply because obedience in the matter was not something I wanted to deal with. She commended me on the other areas of my heeding Christ but contended that partial obedience wasn't enough. Match point.

When I think of the few things God had clearly asked me to do—the things I selectively glossed over—I realize now that they were not terribly logical moves, which made them difficult (like the servants bringing water when the wedding needed wine). And, come to think about it, forget logical, how about plain uncomfortable? Hard? Painful? Scary? He was asking me to make changes in some of my relationships that had become "ultimate things." The only problem was that these changes required steps I didn't think I could make but absolutely needed to for freedom. He wasn't asking for a flawless, triple salchow performance, but a heart agreement and a willingness to respond to the brim. When I finally decided to obey him in full measure, to step away from a few things that, looking back, were actually tying me up in far more ways than I understood at the time, I began to experience the peace that accompanies obedience.

God wanted everything from me, not just the obedience that made sense. It was not a matter of picking and choosing but of surrendering my will to him and agreeing to do things his way, regardless of the discomfort. It was a really tough choice at the time, one that was far from smooth or walked out cleanly. I remember the shrill of loneliness and the tearstained pages of journaling, though something underlay my journey that granted sweet stability beneath my steps. It was an immovable peace that accompanied my obedience and eventually surmounted my discomfort. I wasn't perfectly at peace at all times, but the obedience itself cast my road in a restful hue.

My conversation with Barbara and the ensuing clarity and conviction happened a few years ago. Enough time has whipped by for me to have at least some partial understanding of the changes God wanted me to make, the areas in which he wanted me to heed him. What I once viewed as miserable, I now see as lifesaving obedience. God has filled in the blank spaces and has done a little water-into-wine switcheroo in the process. Heeding Barbara's advice, which was actually God's command, is not something I would trade for any of the unhealthy but familiar patterns I decided to leave behind. There is simply no comparison to the freedom and blessing Christ has poured upon me as a result of choosing to live by his perfect law of liberty.

Though the Lord has set my feet on wide and solid ground, getting here was not pretty. The process was a messy effort on my part, one that manifested itself in some knock-down-drag-out fights with the people I loved, a few pouty months with the Lord, and an overall sloppy walking out of the whole thing. But it was total. And if I can be so presumptuous, I believe God was pleased.

# (15)

# SNOW DAY

Given that I was often leading worship in Ft. Lauderdale much of last year, I spent a lot of time with the pastor's wife, Lisa, a modeling agent from Miami. Something about the modeling agent piece told me this would not be church as usual. I've met a lot of pastors' wives in my life, and none can switch between fashion and 1 Timothy as effortlessly as Lisa. She's quite a happening really.

Because I got to be such dear friends with Lisa and her husband, David, I was thrilled to hear recently that Victoria, their five-year-old, had asked Jesus into her heart. That's an interesting phrase we Christians have adopted. It basically means that Victoria, with her young mind and budding heart, decided that she needed Someone bigger than herself to enter her life, Someone even greater than her parents to look over her. It means that on some level she understood that she was a sinner, probably because she had said things like "shut up" or had hauled off and hit Charlie, her brother, at least once; and then there were those times when she had shaded the truth about something, like where all that Halloween candy went. It means that in some elemental way she grasped the concept of needing forgiveness for these things and understood that Jesus is the only One who can ultimately offer that to her. It means that she wanted in on the relationship with the Savior whom her family and church had been talking about since she could formulate thoughts. I imagine all of these were wrapped up in Victoria's decision for Christ to come into her heart, and I'm so glad she asked him.

When Lisa called to tell me the news, she said she would catch me up later on all the lovely spiritual aspects of the story but only had time for the humorous strand. Apparently just a few hours into Victoria's remarkable conversion she had forgotten that Christians go to bed when their moms tell them to. Lisa had tucked Victoria in no fewer than the amount of times needed for a pagan child when Victoria called out for "just one more thing." It's been my experience that kids learn this phrase right after the words *mommy*, *daddy*, and *no*. It's negotiation at its finest—seriously, what caring adult can possibly neglect just one more, eensy, weensy, teeny, tiny thing?

Increasingly frustrated, Lisa returned to the room several times, the last being when Victoria asked for more water, which is so great, because kids absolutely never ever ask for water, not even in the desert, except when it's bedtime and there are no further recourses to be tried. Suddenly water is at a premium. I have to say that I can't believe Lisa already used this card—her one ace that she could have saved for some pivotal moment in Victoria's teen years—but, alas, Lisa folded only seven hours into the whole postconversion. She said, "Victoria, you're a Christian now. You need to do what Mommy says and go to bed."

Just short of swooning with the back of her hand gingerly resting on her forehead, Victoria sighed in a wilting tone, "Being a Christian is *so* hard!"

Regardless of what else Victoria has grasped so far about the Christian life, she has indeed taken hold of a prominent truth. Being a Christian is hard primarily because it requires a death to ourselves. Our flesh with all of its powerful desires has to be crucified, our idols have to be deconstructed, and we get to do this thing called surrender and submission, which goes against the just one more thing in all of us. And because none of us does this flawlessly we have the—to be celebrated—discipline of God. It is our aid to holiness, the sometimes painful guide to wholeness and life.

o   o   o

I was reading in Romans chapter 15 this morning when I noticed Paul's claim to speak only of the things Christ had accomplished through him. (He was talking about how God had used him to reach the Gentiles with his ever-extending grace.) For me, it was a reminder that if there's anything that's been accomplished in me in the last few years it's been this issue of obedience being worked out in an otherwise determined-to-do-it-my-way-thank-you-so-much kind of girl.

This all wouldn't be so hard if I didn't have award-winning flesh.

It is of Olympic caliber, which makes it so much more painful to beat. My dad loves to tell the story of when I was three years old and had been the proud recipient of so many spanks in one afternoon he had lost count. Although I don't remember such defiance, my dad promises that after one particular swat I looked him resolutely in the eye and said, "I don't know why you keep spanking me, cause I am not going to obey." I think this meant at least one more spank in my future.

Interestingly enough, I have changed my tune now that I am in my thirties and am frankly tired of a stinging bottom. I am all about obedience. Not every time, and not nearly as quick as it should be, but obedience is high on my list of priorities. I'm pretty sure it has something to do with the God-sized spankings I've gotten, which spare your butt but will break your heart in half. And though at times it's agonizingly painful, I am ever grateful for God's discipline in my life, especially when it comes to the lesser things I have put in place of him.

Hebrews 12 speaks of God's deep love for his children, which can sometimes seem cloaked when delivered in the form of discipline. The writer of Hebrews encourages us to take heart during seasons of God's rebuke because he disciplines those he loves. The passage also reminds us how much we ultimately respect our parents for correcting and chasing after us, even though we may have screamed and wailed and wanted to swing back with our own paddle a time or two.

The blessing of Hebrews 12 is that it goes on to say that God's discipline is for our good. And this is precisely what's really easy to miss because it feels so doggone painful. God's dealing with us can seem unbearable at times, even torturous, and anything but for our prosperity.

Yet it is for our benefit, our blessing, our joy. It is not for the sake of legal-istic living. It is not for our destruction. It is not so we can turn our gaze heavenward and say, "I don't know why you keep doing this, cause dang it, I am not going to obey!"

There is no doubt that some of the most painful times in my life were during seasons when God was dealing with my idols. We remember that the Ten Commandments commence with having no gods before him. The author of these life-giving tenets will only stand by so long. He will not let the children he loves enough to offer up his own Son destroy themselves with lying gods that promise what they can never fulfill. He'll only let us stick our finger in the light socket so many times.

o    o    o

I remember when I was in high school and had made friends with some older kids on the wilder side. They were all a year above me, which is only important because it was that critical year that separates drivers from nondrivers, cool from not cool, royalty from serfs. Unless of course you had friends who could drive, which made you honorary cool. The only hiccup on my road to coolness was that my mom wouldn't allow me to drive with any of these particular sixteen-year-old friends because she didn't think it was safe. This was pure and simple torture. She might as well have strung me out back and thrown Lacey's (our beagle's) food at me twice a day as far as I was concerned.

One wintry morning during geometry a thick gray sky opened its hatch and down came enough snow to release us from the torture of learning. Why I reasoned that a pile of snow and an early dismissal would somehow override my mom's rule of no driving with these particular people, I cannot recall. When my friend Steve asked if I wanted a ride to my friend Kerry's house, I was engulfed by a sea of freshmen and sophomores scrambling for their loser buses. It was my one chance to proudly saunter past the bus line and wave to my classmates while throwing my stuff in the back of Steve's Bronco II. In view of all that was at stake, I didn't feel that my mom's rule was holding its own too well. With a quick "sure!" I suddenly became queasy, certain I had done a bad thing but hoping that the greater good of popularity would win out in the end.

We were no more than a block from our school when Steve hit his brakes and his car did the most unexpected thing in snowy conditions, which was to glide full speed ahead until it slammed into the car in front of us. As we all sat there stunned, I became far more afraid of what my mom was going to do to me than I was of whiplash or bruised ribs or even amnesia.

All I remember thinking was how much trouble I was going to be in, how God was punishing me. In my legalistic reasoning, I was sure that everyone was in the wreck because of my disobedience. I understood little of God's grace at the time and was confused about his discipline. It wasn't about ordaining a fender-bender on Sutton Road because I crossed my mom or about scaring me into relationless obedience. God's discipline was, and is, about his love for me. It was vital for me to learn that God's principles and commandments are not arbitrary ideas he comes up with to make us as uncool and miserable as possible.

He has infinite reason behind wanting us to be obedient, even when it means breaking off an unhealthy relationship, or turning off a racy television show, or getting on the lame bus.

Besides a little soreness the next day, we were all fine, which I'm grateful for to this day. I can't remember what my mom said (or did) to me, but I remember the lesson of obedience more vividly than the accident itself. Mostly, I began to catch the principle of discipline as affection.

It's like walking behind a toddler on the sidewalk. I've noticed they zigzag a lot, following whatever whim they please, their attention constantly robbed by sounds and objects. I find myself having to cup them with my body, cutting them off on either side, creating an imaginary hem along their path. It is not out of meanness or cruelty that I keep them from the fascinating bright yellow truck that's tearing down the street, or from the sweet furry dog that's salivating on its chain. Occasionally the word *no* must be spoken, and there are tears and full-on meltdowns on the sidewalk. They don't understand this form of love, the kind that constricts and restrains. Hebrews 12 asks the lovely question, how much more then is God's discipline perfect and full of love.

If you are in a season of what feels like God trouncing your every move, if you can't get away with a thing, and if the leash you're on feels painfully short, perhaps you are in a season of discipline, of God dealing with a false god or two. One way you can know it for sure is if everyone around you is doing all the same things you're doing but is walking away free and clear, seemingly blessed. That's when you aggravatingly know the Lord's got his hand on you—the one you wish he'd move onto someone else, though in reality that would be the most tragic thing that could ever happen. Because discipline is not rejection, it is protection and affection, one of the most glorious things God can extend to us.

○ ○ ○

I am reminded of Hosea 2, of God's discipline of an adulterous wife who represented the idolatry of God's people. She had gone after other lovers, false gods, never understanding that it was God who had brought her the blessings that surrounded her. Because she represented his children, he couldn't allow her to prosper on such a rebellious path. So in Hosea 2:6–7 (KJV) the Lord says, "Therefore, behold, I will hedge up thy way with thorns, and make a wall, that she shall not find her paths. And she shall follow after her lovers, but she shall not overtake them; and she shall seek them, but shall not find them: then shall she say, I will go and return to my first husband; for then was it better with me than now." This is what happens when God is our Savior and we are his children and we head off the path (or even when we are following him but need refinement). We get thwarted. As his children, we don't have the freedom of rejecting his instruction long-term.

If you are in a season where God is dealing with your idols, I hope you will take the full course. Don't despise it. This truth has been a great healer to me, albeit a surprise. After going through some deep disappointments and rejections—one being when I first came to Nashville and struggled so painfully as an artist—I realized that those difficulties were not God's anger—or worse, his indifference—but his refining power manifesting itself in my life. It was his discipline that was renewing me, knocking the legs out beneath my idolatry while revealing himself as the sole authentic lover of my soul. Let him have his way, let him do his sweet work in you. It is not for reckless unkindness but for the beautiful process of transforming you into the image of Christ. Receive his discipline, not as rejection, but as chosen affection.

# (16)

# ISHMAEL MOMENTS

Wrapped up in the foundational concept of obedience and discipline is the beauty of surrender. It's the safest, scariest thing we can ever do, relinquishing ourselves and laying down our rights, wills, and dreams before our Redeemer. I have surrendered much at the feet of his supremacy, yet in God's mysterious economy he always restores more than I have ever given up in the first place. This goes for the good things we put before him (what we'll refer to as our Isaacs, after the promised son of Abraham and Sarah), as well as the inherently fleshly things we lay at his feet (what we'll refer to as our Ishmaels, after the son Abraham had through Sarah's slave girl, Hagar).

I believe that before we can ever lay down our Isaacs we must first lay down our Ishmaels. Though we will touch on the pivotal story of Abraham and Isaac, I've found it essential to first visit the offering up of Ishmael. No wood, no fire, no stone, no cruel knife—but a critical offering of the heart nonetheless. Yes, there was that great sacrifice of Isaac. But first, there was Ishmael.

I frequently have to offer up my flesh—those raw self-centered longings that stand in contrast to the liberating lead of the Spirit. (Remember that in the Bible Paul uses the word *flesh* not for our physical nature but for our lower, self-obsessed nature. Paul is not at odds with the fact that we're physical creatures with physical needs and desires.)

Occasionally I have an Isaac moment where I've got a knife in the air, poised to offer the very thing God so divinely gave, willing to plunge into the unfathomable mystery of fearless obedience, even at what appears to be at the expense of God's unwavering promises. Isaac moments. They only come around so often.

Ishmael moments are another thing altogether. I have them every day. They come when I'm deciding between immediate satisfaction and patience, between my will and the Spirit, between my tangible strength and God's miraculous ways. Ishmael is my flesh, he is the law, he is earthly and everything merely human. I have to send him away intermittently throughout my day, sometimes several times per minute. Like Wile E. Coyote who gets blown up fifty times per episode, yet somehow robustly appears in the next frame, so it is with my Ishmaels.

Though we touched briefly on the story of Ishmael in the chapter called "Legalism," it is worth a deeper look from a different angle. As I read the story of Abraham, Sarah, Hagar, and Ishmael, I never cease to be reminded of the pain and destruction I can cause by my own hand. Though their story is ancient, its principles are maddeningly modern: God had promised Abraham and Sarah a son who would lead to many nations and kings. However, as is so often the case with God's promises, the circumstances stood defiant—they were both both extremely old, and Sarah remained barren as night after night set one upon the other.

You can almost hear their desperate words to one another: What about the covenant? What about the promised son? What about all those kings and nations that are to follow? Are we sure we heard God right? Time is running out. History hangs in the balance. Redemption is at stake. Our womb is shut! God needs our help. And somewhere along the line that runaway train of thought led to the fateful words of Sarah: "Abraham, take my maidservant."

We have the luxury of being privy to the whole story when looking at the lives of Abraham and Sarah. We slap our foreheads and cringe, wondering why they ever pulled Hagar onto the scene, because we know that Isaac isn't far off, and we know the nightmare that Ishmael ends up being to Sarah, and how the pain bleeds over onto Abraham. So in our hearts we think, *Come on, you two, hang in there, just a few more years and God's gonna bring out one of his better miracles. You'll get your son, Isaac, and you won't have to suffer through all that domestic drama.*

We plead with them in our minds, but it's only because we've got the whole script in our hands. Sarah and Abraham only knew what they knew at the time, which is that God had promised but nothing had happened. They got discouraged and hadn't yet discovered how swiftly God's hands can move when he's ready, as fast as he summons forth spring.

o   o   o

The suddenness of spring never ceases to remind me of how quickly he can move when it's time. Spring is overnight stardom really, its entrance covered in fanfare. And who wouldn't want to celebrate something that has the monopoly on green? That initial vibrant lime green that pops against a blue sky. It is not the kind of green you find in a box of crayons. Not even the double-decker boxes. It is spring-green, and it is all its own.

Just yesterday spring prompted me to fumble my way down to the local farmers market, and I say fumbled, because I guessed at turns and roads until I finally saw the myriad vendors and plants and blooming flowers. They were playing forties music over the loudspeakers while I dragged my flower wagon around. Spring-green and spring-blue were everywhere, and for just one moment I pretended to be in an old Hepburn movie where the world was well. I was ready for some glorious man to glance at me from across the aisle, piercing eyes finding me through the cutouts of a flower arrangement, asking me if I had dinner plans. Reality snapped me back when none of this even remotely happened, and my three girlfriends yelled at me across the way to pull the car around and help load the arrangements. Not to mention when it came time to plant, and weeds and tree stumps lay where zinnias, petunias, and daisies were supposed to go. Out came the hatchet, soil, and potting gloves. Audrey would have never sullied her hands this way.

I suppose the thing that amazes me most about spring is how lightning quick the whole thing happens. I mean, you have to wait a bunch of months for it, but when it finally hits it's like the circus coming to town. All of a sudden you've got long days of light, exploding color, singing birds, and all kinds of creatures taking to the streets and air. It's a celebration of life where most every strand of nature cries, "Look at me!"

o   o   o

I think Sarah and Abraham were just a little on the front side of spring when they determined Hagar the slave girl was the way to go. They forgot how fast spring happens when it finally dawns. How immediate God's strokes are when he deems it time to move. It was as if they could comprehend the promise but not the fulfillment of it. As time passed, they must have figured it was up to God to come up with the promise but up to them to carry it out. They didn't understand things like "the appointed time."

And so … Ishmael was born.

He is the product of will. The child of all things human. He comes into existence when we can't wait any longer. When we determine for God how he should sculpt his promises. When we get a really good idea and execute our plan before ever asking if it was God's genius or our own. When we just plain want what we want. Ishmael. His name resounds with booming heartache. He represents the functional gods of our hearts, because he is substituted for the promise of God; we rely on him to deliver what only God can provide.

Hagar's pregnancy with Ishmael did not ring in the most seamless of transitions, as you can see firsthand in Genesis 16. There was no baby shower from what I can tell. Hagar seized a coveted opportunity to look down on her mistress, and Sarah loathed her for it. Abraham was caught in the crossfire, balancing both women as best he could. Eventually the scales dramatically tipped when Sarah made Hagar's life so miserable that she fled the scene. Incidentally, Hagar was being punished for giving Sarah exactly what she wanted—a pregnancy. The only problem was that I guess it wasn't what Sarah thought, or how she thought, and so her great mistreatment of Hagar sent her slave packing.

She couldn't stay away too long, however—that whole angel-appearing-to-you-in-the-middle-of-the-desert thing will get you every time. At the moment of her desperation, an angel of the Lord showed up and encouraged her to return home. This appearance came with a couple of questions slightly weightier than how would you like your eggs? Questions like "Where have you come from and where are you going?" while you're pregnant in the empty desert and suffering from a splitting heart—they're enough to make anyone consider a change of direction. With angelic grace and transcendent eyes, the angel of the Lord sent her back home.

No one was getting off easy. Everyone was going to have to make this work, at least for a time. Sarah was going to have to stop hating Hagar, Hagar was going to have to stop mocking Sarah, Ishmael was going to have to grow up as though he were Isaac—the most impossible task of all—and Abraham was going to have to figure out a way to live peaceably between both women. Not exactly a Brady Christmas.

Scripture doesn't so much as crack a window into the next thirteen years of what is beginning to look like a regular Western dysfunctional family. We get no further insight into the dynamics of nightly gatherings around the dinner table, family vacations, or the harrowing prospect of a husband trying to appease a barren wife and a fertile mistress. We are left to our imaginations to sketch the inevitable jealousies, heartbreaks, and entangling web that must have engulfed their home. These are the untold years of Ishmael's life.

We don't get any more detail until God appeared to Abraham in Genesis 17, right around Ishmael's thirteenth birthday. God rehearsed many of his earlier promises to Abraham about making him into a great nation and giving him a son from Sarah's womb. Though I'm always prepared for a relieved and enthralled Abraham at this point, Scripture tells a different story. The picture given is one of Abraham literally falling to the ground in laughter over the thought of having a child with Sarah. In the confines of his heart he secretly mused how a hundred-year-old man and a ninety-year-old woman could have a child. (He has a point.) But if we follow Abraham's shock to its logical conclusion, we arrive at a most interesting end.

Abraham must have thought Ishmael was the promised heir.

If the prospect of having another child caused him to roar with laughter, he was left with Ishmael as his only possible succession. How easily we sell God short. How often we comprehend the promise but assume it's up to us to fulfill it. And then when we do fulfill it by our own meager means and bare hands—which is really no fulfillment at all—we are stunned to find that our crude model, which bears nothing of the miraculous, is surprisingly not the promise. It's a really good Ishmael, but it's not an Isaac.

The astonishment in Abraham's heart is interesting to note, but it's the words that actually came from his mouth in the next moment that have affected me to this day: "If only Ishmael might live under your blessing!" (Gen. 17:18).

"If only Ishmael might live under your blessing!" Let this settle for a moment.

When I first grasped the gravity of this phrase, I had never before considered Abraham's deep love for Ishmael. His attachment. The child's reality for thirteen years. We give so much attention to the written story of the great sacrifice of Isaac on Mount Moriah, but what about the unwritten story of Ishmael? Genesis leaves us virtually nothing to go on but this one steely cry of Abraham's heart. And it is all we need.

o   o   o

A few weeks ago, my friend Mary Katharine invited me to go play with some kids under the age of four, all belonging to a friend of hers. I wasn't terribly keen on the idea but was afraid I was becoming one of those selfish single people, so I did it in the noble name of sacrifice. Off I went into kid-land. After pulling into the driveway, I maneuvered through a maze of trucks, tricycles, dolls, balls, and some toys I'd never seen before, which means anything invented past the turn of the century. I followed the screams into the backyard like in the cartoons when someone is looking for food and that squiggly line strings them along until they eventually wind up at something really good like a blueberry pie.

There they were. Flailing around like kids do. Giggling, screeching. Toppling over one another in a pile of kid-ness. But, of course, as soon as we showed up, they were no longer contented with their fun selves but were now in need of grown-up attention, someone to flip, swing, chase, and kiss them. Actually, the kissing part is my own demand. I consider it part of their reasonable service to offer their chunky baby cheeks to me for smooches.

After one forty-five minute visit I was smitten. Smitten, I say. Last month I had never conceived of these kids and now I find myself, on a regular basis, singing songs about kites and the atmosphere, lifting little bodies up one at a time to hang from trees, and swatting at invisible piñatas. I converse about dense topics like make-believe characters, and wear purple party hats, and am tempted to leave fifty bucks per visit at their mother's door for the pure therapy that it is.

Is it unreasonable for me to think that Abraham's affection for his own son would be a million times stronger than my budding care for my new little friends? I can't conceive of the love I would have for a child coming from my own body—one who had been with me for thirteen years. When it comes to Abraham's story, I have to remember that he hadn't even imagined Isaac when he was asked to relinquish Ishmael. Again, because we know the whole story, it's easy for us to pass over his heartache, knowing the blessing of Isaac was just around the corner. But Abraham was already attached to Ishmael. He wasn't necessarily interested in getting excited about someone else he had yet to meet or even dream of.

"If only _____ might live under your blessing!" What is your own plea?

"If only this man who is not my husband might live under your blessing. If only my love for alcohol, my jealousy, my compromising addictions, my secret lusts, my workaholism, this tiny emotional affair, or something entirely good but not best—if only it might live under your blessing!"

Have you ever wished such things? Ever longed for what felt right to be right? There are so many things in my life that I just want so ding-dang bad to be okay with God. There are people and desires and propensities and things I've already got in place that I just want to live under God's blessing. Habits I've tended to and desires I've caressed, yes, Ishmaels I have raised. But God, in his infinite kindness and understanding, says, "No, it must be *this* way."

But his words don't end here. He shows us his graciousness and spares us from the ever-popular-with-moms quote, "Because I said so." Although he has the right to use these words as he wishes and sometimes does, he refrains in this instance. Instead, in his profound mercy, he whispers to Abraham, and to us, "As for Ishmael [fill in your blank], I have heard you" (Gen. 17:20).

Has God heard you? Have you carried your Ishmael to him? I'm not talking about your Isaac, but your Ishmael. Carried the product of your will, the consequence of your unbelief, the child of your rebellion? The idol of your heart? Have you admitted to God your deep affection for the things not born of his promise? The things you love to love but are afraid might not be able to exist before him. Have you cried out from the depths of your heart, "If only _____ might live under your blessing!"

God so delicately continued on with Abraham in regard to Ishmael: "I will surely bless him; I will make him fruitful and will greatly increase his numbers.... But my covenant I will establish with Isaac" (17:20–21).

I take great comfort in this dialogue between Abraham and God, as it shows how clearly he hears our desires. It extends an invitation for us to freely take our longings and attachments to him, even the ones that are of Ishmael proportions. We find that he's in touch with our longings. He grieves with us over our attachments. He has grace on our Ishmaels, and yet he is unwilling to allow them to ever take the place of Isaac. No, what is born of our flesh can never substitute for what is born of the Spirit. God's glory and our freedom are at stake, and he won't think of compromising either.

# (17)

# A LONG WALK

On the road to relinquishing our idols, this offering up of our Ishmaels is essential. There is really no glossing over this step—before Abraham could ever offer up the child born of the miraculous, he first had to offer up the child born of his flesh. So it is with us.

I have fresh memories of dealing with my own Ishmaels before God. I remember a day when things in my life had hit such a point of pain and chaos that my single recourse was to get out of the house and walk, perhaps to a different state. Nature and its untouched air seemed so grounding compared to the continually shifting surface on which I had been living. Being outside amid creation felt settling and secure, a place to move around and spew adrenaline and questions into the open air. Mostly the outdoors offered a clear space to wrestle things out with God.

I didn't know where else to start with him than at the honest core of my feelings. This was no time for offering up to God what I was supposed to be feeling or what I thought he wanted to hear, like when a question is pointed at five-year-olds in Sunday school class and the answer is always Jesus, even when the question is something like "What's your favorite color?" I had to give him the real deal, the true plea of my heart, the "if only _____ might live under your blessing" cry. Plus, I know God is not afraid of my genuine feelings, nor is he ignorant of them. For him to have any shot at transforming them, I have to at least give up pretending that they aren't what they are. All the stuff inside me needed to be changed, not dressed up or avoided.

So I began by rehearsing my love for my Ishmaels. Not literal children running around, but things I desired and tended to that were simply not of God. They were the things that you know in Scripture, know in your heart, and know by the Spirit living inside you cannot exist in your life; and yet they can live and breathe by the oxygen of excuses and justifications for quite a long time—surprisingly long I might add. They are the things we all have—in different forms of course—that sometimes we are blinded to, while other times we are downright convicted by.

In my case, I think I justified my disobedience with blurry vision for a while, but eventually I lost out to the clarity of the Holy Spirit. One of my Ishmaels was jealousy and its consequences. It had roared up within me while I allowed myself to be swept up in its current into unwise decisions and reactions. I had been overlooked in an area that made me feel rejected while another person seamlessly slid into my place. However, I had to agree with God that allowing jealousy to dictate my path only dug me a hole worse than the original pain of what hurt me in the first place. As we saw earlier, my jealousy was a helpful arrow that pointed to a lack of trust that God could make up for what I had so unjustly lost. The Lord had not missed my anguish and was indeed able to sustain me through the hardship, even working all the pain for my greater good.

While walking with God, I rehearsed my attachments to the things I knew he was calling me to relinquish, the functional gods of my heart that seemed so promising upon introduction: career paths that could not suffice me, people who could not save me, starry-eyed success that eluded me. Indeed, I had echoed something close to Abraham's words—that Ishmael could just stay—wishing that God and I didn't have to change everything up so drastically. Couldn't he just wave his God-wand and cover my existing path with the blessing?

I had some sad and angry tears with the Lord over the whole thing while expressing my plea. I kicked around some pinecones and crunched the dried autumn leaves beneath the soles of my tennis shoes, frustrated tears lining the path behind me. God proved as patient as he was with Abraham, kindly letting me toss and turn in my emotions before him. He waited and watched, and little did I know, he listened, though I don't think I was as convinced of this until much later when I began to see him do the things that stilled those exact cries.

o   o   o

The morning of my walk I had read Isaiah 44:20, which poetically reads, "He feeds on ashes, a deluded heart misleads him; he cannot save himself, or say, 'Is not this thing in my right hand a lie?'" It was this verse that had prompted me out of the house to take care of the deceit I was clutching like a rag doll. I knew it was time for me to renounce the lie in my hand, even though it never felt so much like a lie. But lies never do; it's funny how they can feel so much like the truth but just a little better. I was tired of being dragged around by a misguided heart, famished by the crumbs of my gods. I was ready for something a little different, yet I wanted all this while keeping what was in my hand. Wish it had worked out for me.

After recounting my desires to the Lord, I knew I needed to take the whole thing a step further: I needed to agree with his truth. Though there wasn't so much as one cell in my body that was happy about it, agreeing with him was essential for change—it was the only starting point for freedom. As I lumbered down the road, both real and symbolic, I spoke into the silence. "Lord, I'm holding a lie. I'm serving a false god. I want to let it go and I want to align myself with where you're leading. I want your truth and I choose to agree with you." Come to think of it, I might have even mumbled these words like a kid who's learning how to say he's sorry. You clearly get the I'm sorry for _____ part, but the rest turns into a mishmash of stuff you can't really make out. To agree with God this way didn't necessarily feel good, but it felt right.

I had to size up my longings with his Word, rehearsing the truth that he is God and that no person has the power to satisfy or save me.

I had to surrender myself to the truth that he would provide for my needs and would give me the desires of my heart—that *he* would do it, not that jealousy was the answer for salvaging what I wanted. I had to agree with him that it is better to serve than to be served, that humility is superior to being celebrated as a well-known success, and that truly, God desired to give me the desires of my heart. But that was something he had to do, not something I could manipulate.

Though I imagine it's as possible for God as spring, I did not discover release instantaneously. Instead, this was the beginning of countless choices, both seemingly insignificant and weighty, that eventually led to freedom. But I did discover it. I am living in it now, and freedom has never been sweeter. I know its roots lead back to that pivotal moment of agreeing with God, of reluctantly bending my wayward self into alignment with his truth. It was agonizing for no other reason than that it required a little more of me to die—the flesh part of me that gets along with the Spirit about as well as our political parties; unfortunately, there is no bipartisanship between these two.

o   o   o

Abraham had to have this aligning moment with the Lord where he embraced God's plan instead of his own. He had to go a step beyond pleading for Ishmael and accept the plan God had for Isaac. This moment wasn't played out until Sarah finally gave birth to Isaac, when the promise became a tangible reality that could cry and sneeze and look around. Suddenly it became clear, to Sarah first, that

Ishmael and Isaac could not coexist; the child born of the slave and the child born of the promise were not compatible siblings. (This is not a commentary on social class separation, but is a symbolic picture of the curse of the law versus the freedom that is found in Christ.) Once Sarah realized that Ishmael was mocking Isaac, she demanded that Abraham send Ishmael and Hagar away, citing that Hagar's son would never share in the inheritance with her own. This was agonizing to Abraham, as Genesis 21:11 describes: "The matter distressed Abraham greatly because it concerned his son."

It's easy to forget that Ishmael was Abraham's son, as we always attribute that position to Isaac. But up until Isaac's arrival, Ishmael was all Abraham had. He loved him deeply, and the thought of sending him away was heartbreaking. This was not an easy matter, perhaps not any easier than the day he leaned over Isaac with a knife in his hand. I'm not sure Abraham would have ever gotten to that point with Isaac if he hadn't first been obedient in this instance. He has become famous for what he parted with on Mount Moriah, but what about the sacrifice of Ishmael that took place so many years before—the one he never got back? Yes, he now had the newborn Isaac to rock in his arms, but he'd had thirteen years with Ishmael, his only son up until that point.

But because this is a picture of bondage versus freedom, the two could not live together. Once Isaac arrived on the scene, a separation became inevitable, much as on my walk with the Lord when I finally concluded there was no way to serve both his agenda and my own. One had to give, and it was either going to be his the easier way, or mine the triple double dog hard way. And so I relinquished my Ishmael, the things

I'd been doing by my own hand and will while hoping that an Isaac, something freeing and miraculous, was on its way.

While Abraham agonized over Sarah's demand to send Ishmael away, the sweet voice of the Lord met him yet again on this matter. "Do not be so distressed about the boy and your maidservant. Listen to whatever Sarah tells you, because it is through Isaac that your offspring will be reckoned. I will make the son of the maidservant into a nation also, because he is your offspring" (Gen. 21:12–13). This is pretty much the same conversation God and Abraham had had a year before, but sometimes we just need to be able to talk these things out more than once, and sometimes the timing is just a little premature the first time for us to really understand. It's like the Lord needed to prep him ahead of time.

o  o  o

Just this past Saturday morning, I was at home peacefully nestled between my covers and pillows—a sad rarity these days. It's not that I don't have time off, just hardly ever on a coveted weekend. I was so excited about sleeping in on a Saturday morning I was almost willing for Friday afternoon to dissipate into the evening so I could slip off into sleep with the knowledge that I wasn't heading for the brick wall of an alarm clock on the other side, but instead could look forward to an open-ended sky of blissful rest. At 7:30 a.m., my phone rang. It was the one thing I forgot to turn off. It was April calling me from the Music City Marathon being held a few blocks away. She had ridden her bike down to 12th Avenue to watch and cheer on the runners. The first words out of her mouth—at an exuberantly high level I might add— were "Next year we have *got* to run this thing!"

It took me a few seconds to form my words, but I remember them being something like, "Okay, but *this* year, I am sleeping."

And so when the Lord had visited Abraham the first time about Isaac, it had been like an early phone call about the following year, a precursor to the event, a little prep work. But when we find him speaking to him this time, the whole thing was in motion. The tangible child, Isaac, had arrived and Abraham was faced with having to let his other one go. And so the Lord visited him with a sweet word, one that lifted Abraham's head with the encouragement that he was going to take care of both sons and that because of this graciousness, he didn't need to be mournful.

Having experienced my own painful losses—some by my own hand and some innocently—I feel that the Lord's voice in these times is an essential accompaniment to the process. There is no substitute for his words spoken over my life, nothing that comes close to carrying the same comfort, weight, or dependability. Several months after my pivotal walk, the Lord spoke one of these words to me that came in the form of Isaiah 43:18–19: "Forget the former things; do not dwell on the past. See, I am doing a new thing! Now it springs up; do you not perceive it? I am making a way in the desert and streams in the wasteland."

It was a passage of Scripture that I had read many times before, but never in the context of it being specifically for me. At this moment it was as if breath had been breathed into it, its words dancing across the pages and into my heart that so desperately needed them. I could hear the Lord speaking into my life, encouraging me as he did Abraham to lay aside the former things, to stop the hurtful dwelling on what used to be. Not because he wasn't sympathetic to the pain of my journey, and not because he wasn't going to tend to what was so important to me, but because he wanted to do something refreshingly new. He knew that there was no way for me to stand in the old and the new simultaneously, to have my heart and mind in both places at once. He was letting me know that he had seen the relinquishment of my Ishmael and that good things were to come. Promise things. Freedom things. Divine things.

When I look at Isaiah 43:18 up against Genesis 21:11, I see similarities that uncover God's heart toward those who have bitterly let something go for the promise of the new. As the Lord told Abraham not to be distressed, because he had good plans for the sons he loved so dearly, I felt God putting his finger under my chin, lifting my head, and saying, don't mourn this any longer. There are blooms of deliverance and blessing springing up, don't you see them?

It reminds me of another portion of Scripture in 1 Samuel 16, where the prophet Samuel was mourning the failure of King Saul. Samuel had been the one to anoint him, and when Saul disobeyed and turned his heart against God, the Lord rejected him as king. While Samuel grieved over Saul's failure, the Lord said, "How long will you mourn for Saul, since I have rejected him as king over Israel?" He then told him to fill his horn with oil and move on to the next king, who was David.

I connect with Abraham's and Samuel's grief, as well as their desire to remain loyal to people and courses, and not just casually toss something out the window that's not quite working. But sometimes the Lord calls us to something new, and in order to live in the new we must lay down the old. It's a tested truth that the flesh of Ishmael and the promise of Isaac just can't live together any more than Saul and David were able to do it. Sooner or later someone's throwing spears and the other's fleeing the country. It's just so much harder to live this way when the two opposing entities are warring within us. That's why it's essential to offer up our Ishmaels to the Lord, to make room for the new, the promise, the path of freedom. When responding to God's direction, the bitterness of a heartbreaking good-bye can't be compared to the sweetness of a divine hello. It is worth whatever you're still clinging to.

# (18)

# ABBEY ROAD

Most often these divine hellos aren't offered us until after we've said a few hard good-byes. It seems to be part of the faith process, where God asks us to leave some detrimental things behind before we ever know what's around the corner. (Think of Abraham who obeyed God by leaving his home yet didn't know where he was going—see Hebrews 11:8–9.) Good good-byes can sometimes be scary, uncomfortable, painful, heart wrenching, yet these God-inspired good-byes to our false gods open up significant room for God to inhabit the space with stunning strokes of his presence and action. And that is the ultimate purpose of tracing our actions and emotions to our idols, discovering them, and then turning from them—not so we can merely be idol-free, but so our lives may be spacious places for God to dwell and move. It is all about making room for him.

A few years ago I sat in my living room facing what seemed a demising career after getting the news that my second record company was disbanding. It was the final straw in a slew of shocking and unlikely disasters that decorated my every move in the music business. I knew the Lord was asking me to step away from it all, to lay down my own agenda of what my artistry, career, and ministry was to look like. Not because the road had been wildly difficult—that part I could have hung with—but because I finally realized that all those years I had been striving to accomplish things my way, on my terms, by my own strength. The whole thing had become a governing idol in my life, and the Lord was asking me to put it down. I prayed my prayer of relinquishment, crying, angry, doubting God's goodness in my life—but I surrendered nonetheless.

I remember making the calls to all involved parties telling them I was stepping away from the industry aspect of my music, truly with no idea of what would be next. It was a tearful, difficult, and grieving good-bye, but one I was confident I needed to make. The year ahead was paved with piecemeal work, as I cobbled together lawn mowing, writing, fence staining, painting, a little singing, and whatever else my hand could find to do to scrape together income. It was a trying time but a necessary passage that stripped me of what I had been placing my hope in, making room for God to dwell in ways incomparable to what I had been grasping at before. All this with a pressure washer in my hands.

The journey I took with the Lord on this one was long and involved, yet he eventually granted me a picture of what he can do to surrendered dreams. This reckoning brought me to that perfect point on the circle, the one that marks the beginning of the process as well as the completion of it, where you see everything come together and realize that indeed God's plan was for your good, not your devastation.

o   o   o

About two years after this difficult good-bye came an astonishing hello. It was a little surreal. The original gear, the control room, the renowned zebra-striped walkway, the hallways that had been privy to the whispers and conversations of the Beatles. Musical genius and pop culture had been crafted—or stumbled upon—within the very walls where I stood. The understated presence of this place in the quiet St. John's Wood of London bolstered its mysterious and celebrated quality. I felt not so much like a kid in a candy store as an adult in one—I got it, I respected it, I knew what it meant. It was Abbey Road.

I had been asked to be part of a live DVD recording called *Worship from the Abbey,* a worship event produced by Kingsway music group. It included a host of worship leaders from different parts of the world coming together for a night dedicated to bringing glory and praise to our God. It was an unprecedented evening of worship in Studio I (where movie scores are recorded), a venue more apt to house music from *Lord of the Rings* or *Star Wars* than a live audience bellowing out songs about the cross, our need for repentance, and God's holiness. If walls could speak, they would have praised that night.

During the rehearsals leading up to the event, I wandered around Abbey Road like the Narnia children looking for a secret wardrobe or storage closet that might whisk me away into some magical land where "Can't Buy Me Love" or "Here Comes the Sun" was dreamt. A place where I'd play an electric guitar that was plugged into vintage pedals that sang in dreamy and glossy tones, where I'd be supernaturally infused with the skill to play each melody with flawless deft. Instead, I found the in-studio restaurant. Its full-time chefs worked round the clock creating decadent tastings for every palette. They served all day and well into the night, and I'm sorry but who needs a magical wardrobe when you have food? I hate to be so superficial, but as great as the Beatles were, the tiramisu and cappuccino weren't so bad either.

After many escapades from the studio to the café and back, the rehearsals had wrapped up and our evening of worship was finally upon us. It was a truly humbling experience to have some of the finest musicians and singers in the world grace the stage as the house band. Since I had to concentrate only on the one song I was leading, I was afforded the luxury of being able to relax most of the night and engage in some of the sweetest worship I have ever been a part of. From celebratory songs to ones calling for repentance to timeless hymns, the gamut proved rich. And from different colors and races and cultures stood each worshipper onstage, reminding us all of the one day when every tribe and tongue will sing God's praise.

When it was my turn to take the stage, I felt strangely as if the oxygen had been sucked from the room. *How am I supposed to breathe*, I kept thinking. My heart was pounding so hard, like it was nailing a picture to the inside of my chest, and it wouldn't heed my attempts to tell it to settle down already. I couldn't discern if it was nerves, the magnificence of being at Abbey Road, the worshipping crowd, the Holy Spirit rising up inside me, or a fanciful combination of them all, but I was a bit of a wreck. Tim Hughes, a worship leader and writer from the United Kingdom, led a song right before me called "Happy Day," which is about God's grace and forgiveness, and I couldn't help but tour the big landmarks of past sin in my life, almost coming out of my skin with gratefulness that, indeed, he has "washed my sin away."

I felt seconds away from a nervous implosion, but alas, it was time to take the stage, plug in my guitar, and sing one of the greatest hymns of our day, "How Deep the Father's Love" by Stuart Townend. It tells the rich story of God's great love and sacrifice for his people, and our response to such a severe mercy. As we approached the third verse, the worship became palpable, almost something you could reach out and grasp hold of. The band kept building, layering instruments and tones that danced seamlessly with the explosive lyric, "But I will boast in Jesus Christ, His death and resurrection." And when we got to that last word, the word that all Christianity hangs upon, the word that separates it from all other religions, that gives us a God and not just a man—*resurrection*—the whole room erupted in glorious praise.

And as I sang amid that beautiful group of worshippers, I became aware of how great Studio I of Abbey Road was all over again. This time not so much because of its legendary status, but because of who was in our midst. I knew it wouldn't make the papers or hang on the walls or be documented as one of Abbey's most legendary moments, but God had visited us, and I couldn't help the thought that perhaps this was secretly one of its greatest nights few would ever know about.

I went back to my hotel that evening richer: richer for the culture, the musical experience, the coffee, but mostly richer for the understanding of what it means to lay something invaluable down (a good thing that had become an "ultimate" thing). To walk through a bunch of "Where in the world are you, Lord?" seasons and then watch him resurrect the whole thing in an inconceivable way was a little more than I could take in. Never in any dream or thought or state of madness did I ever conceive of getting to sing at such a renowned venue, yet the experience itself paled in comparison to what it all stood for on a spiritual plane. I had gone from trimming trees the year before to singing at one of the most prestigious studios in the world, and none of it made any sense apart from God. He had shown me that divinely inspired good-byes—no matter how excruciating—are always for the sake of supernatural hellos.

I have many other situations where I'm still waiting for Abbey Road hellos, greetings I may not get on the front side of heaven. There have been a few precious things I have laid down that the Lord has faithfully chosen not to give back: some activities I don't get to do anymore, some relationships I miss dearly. Good good-byes don't always mean sweet hellos in the natural realm, but they are always meant for our good regardless, even if that good remains a bit of a mystery from our finite vantage.

My experience in London was a sweet gift and picture of the glorious truth that God blesses obedience, but obedience in turning from our false gods is not a guarantee that God will do exactly what we want, nor is it a vehicle by which we can manipulate him. That would be to miss the point entirely. But it is about relationship with him, about his working all things for our good and doing exceedingly more than we could ask or think, and occasionally all of that lines up in ways that pretty much blow our mind. But even more than granting our grandest dreams, he delights in offering us soul blessings, the deep kind that cannot be disturbed by continually shifting circumstances.

o   o   o

I was reminded of this unshakable blessing last weekend when I sang for a group of women who had recently been released from prison and were preparing for life on the outside as part of a truly remarkable ministry called "The Next Door." I met a woman who had gone through the program years ago and who now found herself in the unique position of being a mentor to women in similar circumstances. I'm not sure I've ever seen someone glow as much as Sheila—she looked like she was plugged into something. My friends Scott and Paige and I talked with her at length about her history as she detailed her thirty years of drug abuse that apparently felt better than living in the pain from being given up as a four-year-old child by her mother. Of course, neither avoiding the pain while high nor facing it raw were long-term solutions that worked out for her. It wasn't until her final stint in prison that she met Christ and began the arduous process of allowing him to heal her pain with the salve of his touch.

Sheila is drug-free, clean as you can be, and remarkably dependent upon Christ for her every move. She lives breath to breath for him and by him, and as she so eloquently stated, "I was busy for the Devil for thirty years, now I gotta work double time for the Lord." Her entire life is about him. It was enviable really.

I drove home with a friend who owns his own business and makes a substantial amount of money. On the way home he said, "We have got to start defining blessing differently." His adamant statement was in reaction to how moved he was by the prospect that though he had a thousandfold more in resources and ease of lifestyle, he found himself jealous of her vibrant spirit and her contagious dependence on the Lord. *That* was blessing.

So whether—in response to your courageous obedience in bidding good-bye to the idols of your heart—you get the Abbey Road hello that surpasses your dreams of the glorious impossible, or you get the hello of a vibrant dependence upon God that you've never before known— like Sheila's—God will always outgive whatever you say good-bye to. It's the business he's in. It's what he does.

I pray you've found it time to say good-bye to the small gods who pretend to wield great power, and you're expectantly waiting for God's sweet hello. No other god can compare.

# NOTES

1. John Calvin, quoted in C. J. Mahaney, *The Idol Factory* (Gaithersburg, MD: Sovereign Grace Ministries, 2001).

2. Ken Sande, *The Peacemaker* (Grand Rapids, MI: Baker, 1991).

3. Richard Keyes, "The Idol Factory," quoted in Os Guinness and John Seel, *No God but God* (Chicago: Moody, 1992), 32–33.

4. *Strong's Concordance* (Nashville: Thomas Nelson, 1980).

5. For decades people have found *Mere Christianity* by C. S. Lewis helpful in this regard. A good book addressed to the doubts and questions of this current generation is *Simply Christian* by N. T. Wright.

6. John H. Sailhamer, *The Pentateuch as Narrative* (Grand Rapids, MI: Zondervan, 1992), 285.

7. "The Ten Commandments," Catechism of the Catholic Church, www.vatican.va/archive/ccc_css/archive/catechism/command.htm (accessed December 3, 2007).

8. See www.biblicalheritage.org (accessed December 3, 2007).

9. Anne Lamott, *Grace Eventually: Thoughts On Faith* (New York: Riverhead, 2007), prelude.

10. C. S. Lewis, *The Complete C. S. Lewis Signature Classics: Mere Christianity* (San Francisco: HarperSanFrancisco, 1952, 2002), 75.

# God and gods?

## Do you worship the One, while serving the others?

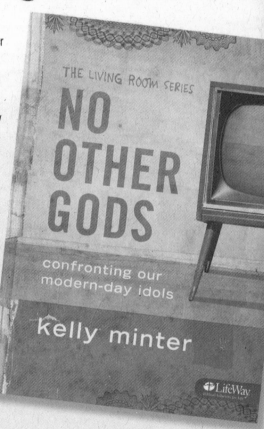